SIM CITY 3000™

Prima's Official Strategy Guide

Rusel DeMaria

Prima Publishing
Rocklin, California
916-632-4400

Table of Contents

Chapter 1
Introduction

FIG. 1-1.

SimCity 3000 is finally here! The crew at Maxis pulled out all the stops with this one. Being in the unenviable position of trying to improve upon the original SimCity and the even bigger-and-better SimCity 2000, they had their work cut out for them, too.

There's little doubt that many of you folks buying SimCity 3000 will be die-hard fans of SimCity Classic or SimCity 2000—in fact, that's part of the appeal of this latest installment in the "urban development simulator." Still, even if you've never played any of these games before, you already have a leg up on the process. Most of us already know a little about cities because we've lived in some kind of village, town, or city at some time in our lives.

We know from personal experience (even if we haven't given it much thought) that people need places to live, places to work, and places to shop. They need ways to get from here to there, and basic utilities, schools, hospitals, and other services. We deal every day with the problems and challenges faced by cities and the people living in them.

We also know from experience that cities are never finished. They never reach some final steady-state and stop changing. Like us, like any living thing, cities change and evolve to survive in a changing environment.

Although we know these things on some levels, it's difficult to grasp intellectually because change happens over the course of years and decades. The urban simulator pioneered by Maxis in *SimCity Classic* allows us to watch this evolution happen in the matter of just a few hours or days. Moreover, because we're in charge, we get to make all the decisions that can take a couple of zoned, empty plots of land joined by a road all the way to a thriving metropolis. On the other hand, we also can make bad decisions that cause people to leave in droves, resulting in a ghost town of abandoned buildings and rusting infrastructure.

FIG. 1-2. A NEGLECTED CITY WILL BECOME AN ABANDONED GHOST TOWN.

Part of what drives change is the development of technology. In the early 1900s, many cities throughout the industrialized world were squalid places, full of pollution, disease, and overcrowding. The advent of the automobile only replaces manure with smog and exhaust fumes. Still, over time, cars became cleaner and more efficient, roads and highways became better, people began making greater use of mass transit, and even the belching factory smokestacks began to be replaced everywhere with high-tech research and office parks.

FIG. 1-3. THE HIGH-TECH CITY OF TOMORROW.

In a parallel fashion, the *SimCity* product line has also evolved, a process possible in large part because the capabilities of the average home computer have made quantum leaps forward at the same time. Processors are hundreds of times more powerful than they were back in the days of the old 8088 or even the 386 CPUs. The tiny little PC speaker has been relegated to the only thing it does well—an occasional beep at power-up—and has been replaced with high-end sound cards and surround-sound speaker systems. Low-resolution 16-color displays are long gone, replaced by 3-D polygon rendering, hardware accelerators, and high resolution at tens of thousands of colors. CD-ROM allows for large, complex programs to be developed and marketed, a big improvement from the days of dozens of installation floppies.

Maxis has built upon the lessons of *SimCity Classic* and *SimCity 2000* to develop a product that makes use of the best of what went before, throws out some ideas that proved awkward or unworkable, and further advances the idea of true "realism" in the design, building, and operation of a city.

However, perhaps you're new to this, and maybe *SimCity 3000* is your first exposure to the idea of an urban simulation. Let's take a few steps back.

What Is SIMCITY?

SimCity, as a basic concept, hasn't changed since its inception. It's an educational product disguised as a really cool game. It's an *urban development simulation* that tries to reproduce with reasonable faithfulness the actual conditions and problems faced by real-world cities.

The urban simulation models real-world conditions and allows you to explore different scenarios and options. In *SimCity 3000*, you can experiment with city planning and layout models as designed by Frank Lloyd Wright and ancient Indian and Greek philosophers. You can try to run cities based on actual real-world examples, such as Paris or San Francisco. You get to work with all of the details, including the dynamic variables of traffic, crime, pollution, and population flux—and do so on a scale ranging from city-wide all the way down to a fraction of what would be a city block.

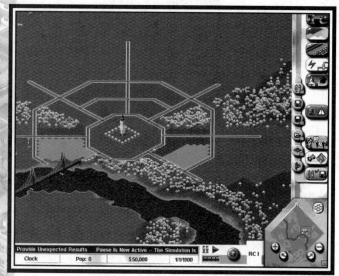

FIG. 1-4. CREATE A CITY OF REGULAR PROPORTIONS OR RANDOM SPRAWL. IT'S YOUR CHOICE.

On top of this, as *SimCity* has evolved, the developers at Maxis realized there were elements of city management they'd left out of the first two incarnations of the game—and many of these newest features were specifically recommended by their customers. For example, subways and expanded options for mass transit were added in *SimCity 2000*. *SimCity 3000* now has you dealing with trash, trying to encourage the transition from dirty to clean industry, and making deals for power, water, and garbage handling with your neighboring cities. Economic models have evolved from relatively simple equations to complex, intricately tunable, robust systems of development.

You're also given active, continuous feedback on your success because of the pace at which the simulation runs. Although you're free to stop the action whenever you want to deal with emergencies, or just to spend some time looking around and deciding what to do next, you're also free to crank up the elapsed time rate and watch months and years zip on by. While this is happening, you can see whether your population is rising or falling, whether buildings are being constructed (and getting bigger and better) or if neighborhoods are becoming run-down and abandoned. You can see for yourself, through your revenue stream and by direct queries, whether your land values are on the rise (resulting in additional funding from property and other taxes) or plummeting. Other features give you still more information if you want it, provided through graphs, budget reports, and news ticker announcements, as well as through the counsel of a team of mayoral advisors and petitioners from within your city and without. You get to find out for yourself whether certain planning decisions take your city in the direction of success or disaster.

SimCity, in all its incarnations, has provided a richly detailed model of urban life and development. The latest version, *SimCity 3000*, takes the concept even further, while at the same time never losing its connection to the past. The whole point of the game is just that: It's still supposed to be a game. In other words, one of the biggest goals is to have fun. The fact that it's also educational is a major bonus.

Unlike many other games, there's no other human or artificial-intelligence opponent for you to defeat. There's no blood-and-gore in *SimCity*, no arcade-style button pushing. Sure, if things go badly in your term as Mayor and you end up too far in debt (more than 100,000 Simoleons of red-ink is what it takes), you can get kicked out of office. Yet, there are no hard feelings. You can always start over or reload a city. *SimCity 3000* offers a noncompetitive, ever-changing environment in which the only limitations are your imagination.

Where Do I Go from Here?

Good question. What you might want to ask yourself is, "Where do I *want* to go from here?"

This book isn't going to duplicate the information you already have in your *SimCity 3000* user manual. We're going to assume you have the game installed and running properly, and that you have some basic knowledge of how to play it. We're also going to assume that if you have a question about how to do something, you can find it either in the user manual or in the online help.

Our goal is to take you behind the scenes, tell you how it all *really* works, so that you can develop better strategies and an understanding of why things happen the way they do in the game. Truly, if you haven't done so already, we recommend you take a few minutes and read through the manual that came with *SimCity 3000*. There's a lot of useful information in there, and you might just realize there's some feature or other you hadn't known about. You might also consider going through the tutorial—especially if you're new to the game, or new to the concept of *SimCity* entirely.

Here, we'll cover some of the basic details of *SimCity 3000*, then get into the individual layers that go into the operation of the urban simulator, and finally provide strategies and pointers for putting it all together.

The following is an outline of what's to come. The beginning chapters introduce the game, describe what's changed (important if you're most familiar with *SimCity 2000*), and help get you started.

SimCity 3000 overview
What's new from other *SimCity* versions
Game settings
Tips for getting started

The second section of the book gets into the specifics of all the citywide issues you'll be watching.

Zoning
Power
Transportation
Water
Pollution and garbage
Public safety, including police and fire services
Demographics, including education and health
How to keep your citizens (Sims) happy
Finances and budget
Ordinances
Neighbor cities
Business Deals
Events
Integration
Tips Summary

Chapter 2
SIMCITY 3000
Overview

SimCity 3000—like all *SimCity* products—is based on certain principles of economics and urban development. You don't have to have a degree in either to enjoy the game, but it does help to understand some of the basics of a *SimCity* economy.

Each of the chapters in the second part of this book deals in some detail with the major aspects of the *SimCity* experience. In this chapter, then, we will introduce the major elements briefly.

FIG. 2-1. CITIES ARE LIKE A LIV-
ING ORGANISM AND GROW OR FAIL
BASED ON YOUR DECISIONS.

The first critical fact to keep in mind is that your city acts like a living organism. It grows and changes constantly. You don't build the city. You only manage its directions and finances. The city is built by Sims—the traditional residents of all SimCities. It's the lives of the Sims that you are responsible for, and if you provide them with good lives, they'll keep coming to your city. If life in your city sucks, then the Sims will pull up stakes and move out. So, right away, you have one feedback mechanism: Is your city growing, shrinking, or staying more or less the same? Under the hood, *SimCity* is a complex set of rules that govern how the city works. There are rules that govern the behavior of Sims. Other rules determine how valuable land is and what will be built on that land. Still other rules affect such elements as crime, pollution, life expectancy, and overall IQ of your population (known as EQ in *SimCity 3000*).

Advisors and Petitioners

FIG. 2-2. CHECK IN WITH ADVISORS AND PETITIONERS FROM TIME TO TIME.

While you're Mayor, you'll have various sources of advice. Some of it comes from your trusted city advisors. Oh, you may not want to follow all their recommendations, but if you're not sure what to do next, check them out. They might have some worthwhile suggestions. Petitioners are citizens of your city (or sometimes the Mayor of a neighbor city or even a representative from a business cartel) who have something to suggest or something to offer. You may want to take what Petitioners say with a grain of salt, but they do come with some important opportunities.

Neighbor Deals, Business Deals, and many ordinances first come to your attention by means of Petitioners. So do special reward buildings like the Mayor's House, the City Hall, and the Mayor's Statue, which are offered when your city reaches certain population milestones. So don't neglect the Advisors and Petitioners window.

The Query Tool

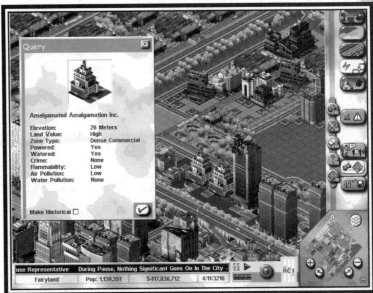

FIG. 2-3. USE THE QUERY TOOL TO SEE WHAT'S GOING ON WITH INDIVIDUAL BUILDINGS AND ZONES.

One of the main menu buttons is the Query tool. When this tool is active, you can click on just about anything in the city and get important information about it. Experiment with the Query tool to see how useful it is. One thing is certain … you'll need it often. Using the Query tool is the only way to get specific information about buildings, and you'll often need to check on the effectiveness of utilities such as power plants, as well as civic buildings like police stations, schools, etc. Many of the chapters in the second part of this book refer to information you can gain using the Query tool.

Time in SIMCITY

Time passes. In *SimCity*, time can pass quickly, or slowly. It can even stop. You control the pace. Sometimes you'll want the city to zoom along so you can get some money in your coffers to do more building. Other times, you'll want it to move very slowly or even stop, so you can micromanage things.

Time also passes in terms of technology. If you start the game in 1900, there are a lot of technologies that simply haven't been invented yet: things like desalinization plants, recycling centers, and fusion power plants. All of it will come in time, but at the beginning, you're stuck with old and limited technologies. You'll want to plan ahead and anticipate that times will change as you play.

If you want to learn more about how events are triggered in *SimCity 3000*, and when certain opportunities may appear, turn to Chapter 18: Triggered and Threshold Events.

Your city may even experience economic cycles as our economy does in the real world. Weathering economic storms may be a part of your *SimCity* experience. That's when it helps to understand more deeply how things work. At the base if it all is the tried and true principle of supply and demand.

Supply and Demand and Land Value

On of the most important rules to understand, true in *SimCity* and in the real world, is the rule of supply and demand—the most basic of economic principles. Demand is measured for each of three types of zones—Residential, Commercial, and Industrial. These zones correspond to houses for Sims, businesses and services, and manufacturing and production. Demand for these zones is created in various ways, but basically, Industrial demand—the demand for manufactured goods—is generated largely from outside your city, though some is internal demand. In contrast, Commercial demand is mostly internal, with some external demand. Residential demand is pretty straightforward and is based on the amount of jobs created in the Industrial and Commercial sectors. Each time a job is filled, there's a Sim who needs a home, which creates a little more demand for housing. To read current demand levels for each zone, look at the RCI graph at the bottom of your *SimCity* screen. If the graph is high, it means there's positive demand. If it is neutral (no color), it means that demand is satisfied for the moment. If it is low, it means negative demand exists and you may want to take measures to help increase that demand.

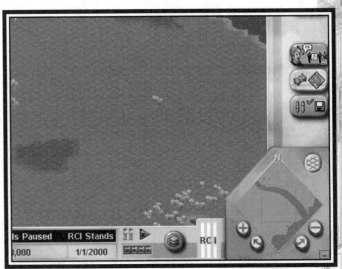

FIG. 2-4. THE RCI GRAPH GIVES YOU AN INDICATION OF DEMAND LEVELS IN YOUR CITY FOR RESIDENTIAL, COMMERCIAL, AND INDUSTRIAL ZONING.

You, as Mayor, decide where to place these different zones and how much land to allocate to them. You can also decide what density these zones should be. There are three densities of zoning—low, medium, and high. The zoning determines what maximum density of buildings can be built, though land value and other factors are considered before any building can take place.

Land value is very important, not only because it determines what kinds of buildings will be constructed, but also because there's a very strong correlation between land value and tax revenue. And, in order to build and maintain a thriving city, you'll need money—lots of it.

For a more complete look at demand (otherwise known as RCI), land values, and land development, see Chapter 6: Land Development and the RCI Model.

Power

Nothing will happen in *SimCity 3000* if you don't provide electrical power. With only a few exceptions, every building and utility in a city requires electricity. So, building and maintaining your power grid is a very important part of your work as Mayor. Chapter 7: Power will give you a far deeper look at how power works in *SimCity 3000*, including a good look at the various types of power sources available to you and their pros and cons.

Transportation

FIG. 2-5. TRAFFIC. IT'S A NECESSARY ASPECT OF CITY LIFE. GET USED TO IT.

Next in importance is the issue of transportation. The Sims in your city are mobile creatures and they must have a way to get from here to there. Primarily, they go from home to work and back, or they may go shopping or out for entertainment. Whatever their destination, Sims must have access to some sort of transportation—whether it's a road or highway on which they can drive their cars, or some form of mass transit like a bus, train, or subway.

One other issue regarding transportation is that Sims won't go very far from their homes or other buildings to find a way to get around. There's a fixed distance that they are willing to go. So, you must keep in mind what Sims require. Don't build their homes far from a source of transportation, and don't make them drive too far to get to work or other places. If you do, you will find that the buildings in your city will start to be abandoned. Sims are easily frustrated if you don't follow the rules.

Also under the heading of transportation are Airports and Seaports, which help keep your Commercial and Industrial sectors healthy and vibrant. You'll need to build Airports and Seaports as your city grows bigger.

For more information on transportation see Chapter 8: Transportation.

Water

Although not quite as critical as electricity, water is something you'll need to provide if you want to have a truly happening, densely populated city. Any source of water on your City Map can be used to provide for your Sims' needs. However, if it's salt water, you'll have to build a water desalinization plant, which may not be available right at the beginning of your game.

You can pump more water using Water Pumps near a water source than any other way, but Water Towers can provide needed city water and can be placed anywhere.

Once you've placed some Water Pumps in your city, you can distribute the output by building a grid of Water Mains. These Water Mains will radiate water for seven tiles on either side. You'll be able to see that they're functioning properly when you go into the special Pipes View.

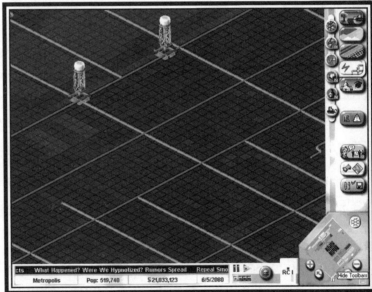

FIG. 2-6. GO UNDER YOUR CITY TO VIEW THE WATER MAINS IN THE PIPES VIEW.

For more information about water, see Chapter 9.

Pollution

Pollution plays a big part in *SimCity 3000*. Most buildings emit some pollution, and some emit a lot. Pollution has many effects on your city—and none of them good. There are three kinds of pollution—air, water, and garbage. Air and water pollution spread from various buildings and can accumulate locally to drive down land values and to mess with the health of your Sims. And, remember, when land values fall, so does tax revenue.

Garbage is a very specific sort of pollution. As long as you dispose of garbage effectively, using landfills or incinerators, you'll have no problems with garbage. However, if you neglect trash collection, your city will, literally, be trashed. Garbage will simply appear everywhere and soon your land values will be plummeting and your Sims will be holding their noses on their way out of town.

For a more complete look at pollution, check out Chapter 10.

Public Safety

Life in SimCity has its dangers. Two principal dangers are fire and crime. Fortunately, there are easy ways to prevent your cities from going up in smoke or becoming crime-ridden slums. Of course, as in real life, in SimCity the solutions cost money.

To combat fire damages to your city, you'll need to build Fire Departments. Each department will have a radius of effect and will also provide a crew in case of emergencies. Thus, the more Fire Departments you build, the more emergency crews will be available if a really bad fire does break out. And make no mistake, fires can and will spread if you don't take appropriate measures.

The obvious solution to the crime problem is to build police stations and jails. police stations, like Fire Departments, have a radius of effect, so you'll have to keep building more as your city grows. Generally, you'll find it worthwhile to keep crime low, because crime can reduce land values and therefore lower your tax revenues. And, anyway, you want your Sims to live long, safe lives.

There's lots more information about fire protection and crime fighting in Chapter 11: Public Safety.

Demographics

What we call demographics are actually the education level (EQ, for Education Quotient) and the overall health (LE, for Life Expectancy) of your Sims. There are various reasons for trying to have your population be more educated and live longer. One of the main considerations has to do with the kind of industry your city builds. Early on, starting in 1900, most industry is very polluting—what we call "dirty" industry. As you already know, pollution has no up side. It's simply bad stuff. Now, it turns out that, over time, technology allows you to develop more and more clean, or nonpolluting, industry. However, clean industry won't develop unless your Sim population is much smarter than they are when they start out. So, you want to raise their EQ by building schools and colleges. Libraries and museums will help keep them sharp.

EQ only grows slowly, and only if you have provided enough schooling to the younger Sims. In effect, young Sims who go through school and college should end up about two EQ points higher than their parents. So it isn't a real fast track to an advanced population. You need to plan ahead, start early, and keep those schools funded.

Hospitals help your Sims stay healthier and live longer. And healthy Sims are happy Sims.

Want to learn more about demographics? Look at Chapter 12: Meet the Sims, Meet Their Needs.

Aura

Aura is a way to see how well you're doing. It's a mood ring for your city. There is local aura, which is affected by crime, pollution, and the presence of desirable or undesirable buildings. For instance, a house built near a beautiful park on the shores of a small lake is going to have higher aura than one built in the shadow of a toxic waste dump.

The second kind of aura is the global "Mayor rating." This is a way to see how well you're doing your mayoral duties, more or less, though there are many ways to see that on your own. If you want to know more, read Chapter 13: City Aura.

Finances

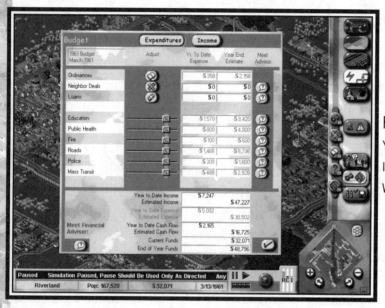

Fig. 2-7. Get familiar with your Budget screens. This is one of the main interfaces with your city.

Yes, as everywhere, money makes the SimCity go 'round. You need money. You'll need to spend a lot, which means you'll need to generate a lot. There are many factors that affect your cash flow in *SimCity 3000*. Your main source of revenue will be taxes, though you may be able to make some lucrative deals with your neighbors to sell them power or water, or even to dispose of their garbage for them—all for a reasonable fee, of course.

You can set specific tax rates for each of your main sectors—Residential, Commercial, and Industrial. Sims are somewhat sensitive to taxes, however, so setting them too high can reduce demand for those zones, while lower taxes, though they don't bring in as much revenue, can have an encouraging effect on development and demand.

SIMCITY 3000: Prima's Official Strategy Guide

Most things in *SimCity 3000* will cost you money. Every zone you place, every building you put down, every road, highway, rail, subway, park, pond, police station, and so on and so forth—they all cost money. And most things also require money every month for maintenance. Most city services, including your transportation network, will cost you in monthly upkeep.

To learn the ins and outs of money management in *SimCity 3000*, read Chapter 14.

Ordinances

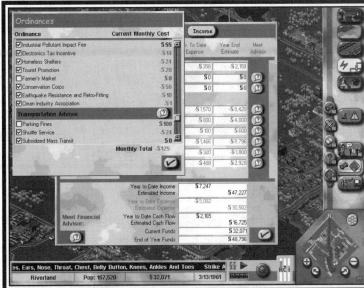

FIG. 2-8. ORDINANCES CAN HAVE A SIGNIFICANT EFFECT ON LIFE IN YOUR CITY.

Besides taxes, which directly affect demand, you can alter the course of your city considerably by passing (or not passing) certain ordinances. Ordinances can have a pretty significant effect on your city, and there are many types. Many of them involve providing some service to the city, and therefore cost money from the city's treasury. A few can actually generate some income, but beware, all ordinances come with some cost. If it isn't money, then it's probably a negative effect. For instance, passing the Legalize Gambling ordinance makes money for your city, but causes a noticeable increase in crime.

You'll learn all about ordinances in Chapter 15.

Neighbor Deals

FIG. 2-9. CONNECTIONS WITH NEIGHBORS CAN OPEN UP A LOT OF POSSIBILITIES.

Your particular city is only one city in a vast, but largely invisible, SimNation. You really never see much of the national picture, but you do have immediate neighbors with whom you can have limited interaction.

You always have four neighbors—basically one in each direction. If you have a land connection, you can build road, highway, train, and subway connections to any and all of them. Building such transportation connections has some very beneficial effects on your city, for a variety of reasons. You'll learn a lot more about transportation connections with neighbors in Chapter 8.

In addition to transportation connections, you can also build power and water connections to neighbors. There are three basic kinds of deals that you can make with a neighbor. You can buy or sell power, buy or sell water, or make a garbage deal that either imports your neighbor's garbage for disposal in your city or exports your garbage to them. All you need to make a garbage deal is one transportation connection (other than a subway) or a Seaport with a connection via water.

Making deals with your neighbors can be very useful. If you need some steady cash infusions, some deals can help your city stay solvent. However, you should read the fine print, so to speak, and understand the pros and cons of each deal. On the other hand, suppose you don't want to put up with the negative effects of power plants, many of which put out a lot of pollution and have other detrimental effects. So, if you have the cash, you can buy all your power from next door and not have to worry about dealing with power plants. It's up to you. Weigh the situation and then go for it.

To learn more, check out Chapter 16: Neighbors.

Business Deals

At various times while you're Mayor, you may be offered some specific business deals, such as the opportunity to build a prison or a toxic waste dump in your city. These deals will always bring money to your city's treasury, but always at a cost. There are ways to soften the negative effects, however. If you understand the workings of these business deals, they can be lucrative. Read Chapter 17 to learn more.

Putting It All Together

Once you understand each of the separate elements of *SimCity 3000*, you'll have a lot of information to deal with. Chapter 19: Puttin' It All Together may help you integrate these elements into a more coherent vision. There are also some suggestions for how to maintain your city and how to deal with problems and situations that may arise.

Tips and Tricks of the Trade

Throughout this book, there are specific suggestions and tips for how to get the most out of your mayoral experience. In Chapter 20: Tips and Tricks, we have attempted to summarize the most important tips to make it easy for you to find them without necessarily reading every chapter.

So, good luck, Mayor. Go have fun.

Chapter 3
This Ain't Your Grandfather's Urban Simulation...

All right, maybe you were a die-hard fan of *SimCity 2000*. Or perhaps you're wondering whether you should buy *SimCity 3000* when that copy of *SimCity 2000* is sitting right there on the discount shelf of your computer software store. Or maybe you're just curious to know what the heck those geniuses at Maxis have been doing with this whole concept of an urban development simulator package.

The fact is, *SimCity 3000* is a whole new game.

Differences between SIMCITY 2000 and SIMCITY 3000

The following table lists the most noticeable feature differences between *SimCity 2000* and *SimCity 3000*.

Feature	SimCity 2000	SimCity 3000
Number of colors	256	More than 64,000, allowing for much more realistic buildings and special effects.
Size of map	128 × 128 tiles	Supports four different sizes: 64 × 64, 128 × 128, 192 × 192, and 256 × 256. *SimCity 2000* maps continue to import into the 128 × 128 map size.
View rotation	Four angles, but not really accurate because the buildings look the same from all angles.	Four fully accurate rotations, with four distinct graphic representations of buildings at each zoom level.
Screen resolution	640 × 480 pixels	Options for 640 × 480, 800 × 600, 1024 × 768—or higher, the only limit being that of your computer hardware. You can see much more of your city in any zoom level with larger screen resolution, although Maxis did keep the needs of more modest systems in mind by making this a scalable feature and by specifically laying the user interface out for each of the primary resolution levels.

Feature	SimCity 2000	SimCity 3000
Animated buildings	A few have smoke and other simple animations	More than 50 buildings with several complex animations, including smoke, neon signs, movie screens.
Sounds	8-bit, with a few sound effects and music	Sophisticated ambient sound effects for the different areas of the city, such as sprinklers in the Residential zones and heavy traffic noise in the Commercial zones. Ambient sound also changes as you scan around your city, reflecting the development and conditions of the areas you are viewing. There are also 14 terrific music scores.
Patterns of development	Completely random within each zone type.	More specific coordination with game states. Which tiles appear, where and when, is influenced by more specific zones, certain ordinances having to do with aesthetics, and the encouragement or discouragement of specific industries. Tiles evolve through construction phases. Agricultural areas appear under certain conditions as a special form of low-density industry. Real-world patterns such as blocks of row houses, commercial strip malls, and subdivision tracts appear based on city game conditions.

Feature	SimCity 2000	SimCity 3000
Avenues	None	If you place two roads next to each other, avenues are automatically created.
Levels of zoom	Four	Five, and the two highest are close enough to show realistic vehicle and pedestrian traffic. The highest zoom level is partly lower quality (buildings) and partly high quality (vehicles, pedestrians, roads, etc.).
Sims	Only shown during riots.	Pedestrians at zoom levels 4 and 5. Sims are small, but capable of general patterns of observable behavior that offer feedback about neighborhood activity— for example, children and strollers near schools, marching soldiers near military bases, picketers during strikes, and panic during disasters.
Terrain	Jagged-edged, terraced for slopes, no change to lighting of tiles when rotated, all undeveloped tiles are plain brown.	More realistic lighting effects, changing with rotation, and a far less jagged, terraced look. The color palette ranges from sand to rocky cliffs.
Layers/filters	Five filters to display different aspects of the city, such as crime, power, pollution, and so on.	Sixteen filters for a more in-depth view of the city, making it far easier to identify trouble areas.

Feature	SimCity 2000	SimCity 3000
User-interface elements	Floating palettes often obscured central activity. Style of pull-down menus was drawn from Microsoft Windows OS standard. No tool tips.	All action buttons are at the edge and do not in any way obscure the city view. Menus have a more contemporary look and are less dependent on the operating system. A news ticker has functionality like that used in Internet browser interfaces. And there are tool tips.
Water pollution and garbage	None	Two new layer components, water pollution and garbage handling add to the challenge of being a Mayor. Garbage visibly piles up if not collected, and water pollution affects the delivery of water to your city.
Undeveloped tiles	Blank colored space	There are filler tiles specific to each zone to fill out the area around and between buildings. These sometimes reflect game conditions— for example, if there's excess garbage, this is where your Sims throw it. There are backyards in Residential areas, fountains in Commercial, and parking lots in Industrial zones. These produce a more realistic look for your developing city and give reasons to zone at different densities, since the results are so varied.

Feature	SimCity 2000	SimCity 3000
Starter towns	A handful of starter towns	Ten small prebuilt layouts are included, based on historically important city planning patterns, from ancient Indian and Chinese city layouts to Frank Lloyd Wright's "Broadacre City" to contemporary designs of the New Urbanists. This allows you to get a quick start into the game by skipping some of the initial planning stages and jumping straight into the fine tuning of the city infrastructure, and also allows you to test these historical city patterns.
News	The daily newspaper	The news ticker, which is continuously present, is modeled on the feature of many Web sites. There are scrolling headlines, some purely informational, some prompting action—for example, clicking on them can lead to an Advisor meeting or take you to the scene of a disaster.
Power and water lines	In *Sim City 2000* there was an elaborate system of laying water and power lines	The process of laying power and water lines has been streamlined.

Feature	SimCity 2000	SimCity 3000
Zone and density types	Two levels of density for each RCI type, low and high	Three levels of density (low, medium, and dense). This version also introduces the notion of a mid-level height cap to buildings, a zoning limitation seen in many cities around the world. There's also a "Historic Preservation Zone" option to lock a designated area and prevent redevelopment.
Puzzle zoning (multi-tile buildings constructed in varying configurations)	Airport and Seaport were the only buildings to use this technique	Technique used more extensively for farms, landfills, and others, including Airports and Seaports. Keeps the visual display fresh and saves on pixel space by recycling tiles in new patterns.
Land value	Simulation component measured by maps and charts	Land value affects taxes directly and the types of buildings that will be constructed on zoned land. This is an emphasized area of strategic play in SimCity 3000. Developers just don't want to build expensive skyrises in bad areas. If you improve your city's land value, you'll see higher-end development taking place.

Feature	SimCity 2000	SimCity 3000
Reward buildings	Five: Mayor's House, City Hall, Statue, Landmark, and Arcologies	Seventeen, including Lighthouse, Country Club, and Spaceport, among others. These are based on different aspects of the simulation, rewarding the different tracks you may emphasize in your city.
Taxes	Simple, only affected the city's budget and the rate of development or decline.	Much more complex. For example, the city's population won't be as forgiving with changes in tax rates over time. Also, land value is factored heavily in determining tax revenues, reflecting the fact that most cities are run primarily on the proceeds of property taxes.
Flora	Trees only, and all of the same bland type.	Different trees at different elevations, and up to five different densities of tree growth possible.
Disasters	Lots of disasters possible.	Fewer disaster types, but handled in a much more realistic fashion. Enhanced mayoral involvement with disaster handling through the Emergency Warning System and budgetary Disaster Relief.
Borrowing money	A "bonds" feature, difficult to use without risking complete financial ruin	City "loans" have been retuned to be a more useful option.

Feature	SimCity 2000	SimCity 3000
Neighbor deals	None	Connect to neighbors and make deals for water, power, and waste disposal, both buying and selling. This allows for a greater variety of strategies for building your city. For example, you can opt to have no polluting power plants in your city whatsoever, but you then get the challenge of managing the budgetary impact.
Business deals	None	Mayors can increase revenue in a pinch by agreeing to site unpopular NIMBY buildings in their cities. Examples include Maximum Security Prison, MegaMall, Casino, and others.
Landmark buildings	None	More 70 real-world landmark buildings, including the Statue of Liberty, Big Ben, the Taj Mahal and more!
Llama Tips or Start Up Tips	None	Offered at the beginning of the game to give you valuable game play hints (can also be turned off).
Aura layer	None	A layer showing your mayoral approval ratings, combining several aspects of the game, including crime, pollution, health, and education.

Feature	SimCity 2000	SimCity 3000
Advisors	Minimal feature buried in the Budget table. Talking heads present short coments in a repetitive manner (80 total messages).	Much more robust and useful. Used extensively to present information, briefings, and options in a personalized and convenient way.
SimPetitioners	None	Sim citizen Petitioners, a new feature, provides opportunities and feedback to you, the Mayor.

Chapter 4
Game Settings

Do you wonder what happens when you pick a particular difficulty level?

Well, you're in luck, because this is where you get the low down on the nuts and bolts: what the simulation keeps track of at each level, what the default settings are, and what the simulation saves when you save your city.

FIG. 4-1. HERE'S WHERE IT ALL STARTS AND WHERE YOU DECIDE JUST HOW MUCH OF A CHALLENGE YOU'RE WILLING TO TAKE ON.

Difficulty Level

There are three difficulty settings in *SimCity 3000*: Easy, Medium, and Hard. These settings affect:

The amount of money you start out with

Easy = 50,000 Simoleons
Medium = 20,000 Simoleons
Hard = 10,000 Simoleons *Loan*

Terrain setting for terraced or smooth landforms

Easy = Terraced
Medium = Terraced
Hard = Smooth

NOTE

WHEN YOU PLOP A LAND-MARK OR CIVIC BUILDING AND THE TERRAIN IS NOT FLAT, IT WILL BE LEVELED FOR YOU AUTOMATICALLY. HOWEVER, THE COST OF THE BUILDING GOES UP IN A MAN-NER REFLECTING THE TERRAIN LEVELING REQUIRED. SO EVEN THE FREE LANDMARKS WILL COST YOU MONEY IF YOU TRY TO PUT THEM ON A HILLSIDE.

City Start Defaults

If you just take the *SimCity 3000* defaults, here's what you get:

Medium difficulty level
Start date is 1900
Terrain Grid is set to ON
Simulation speed is at PAUSED, including when you first load a city
The specific simulation speed in the PLAY setting is saved, so that when you press the Play button after a given city is loaded, it plays at the speed it was playing when saved
For brand new cities, although it starts PAUSED, when you press Play, it defaults to the first speed level
Auto "Go To" is ON
Disasters are ON
Auto Budget is OFF

If you haven't yet set funding levels, but turn on Auto Budget, the budget amounts default to 100 percent levels

Tip of the Day is ON

Music, Sound Effects, and Ambient Sounds are all set to ON and volume set to full

In the Graphs Window, the selected items are City Size, Power, and Funds

Further, at start-up, *SimCity 3000* autodetects and establishes settings for performance-based options (although you can override these):

Traffic visible: Zoom levels or OFF

Other animations: ON or OFF

● Screen resolution depends on detected system performance

● Sims visible: Zoom levels or OFF

Music: Stereo or 3-D Surround

3-D Sounds: ON or OFF

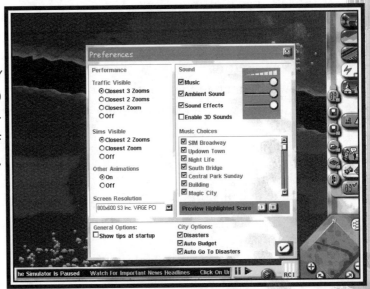

FIG. 4-2. YOU CAN TUNE *SIMCITY 3000*'S GRAPHIC AND SOUND OPTIONS TO SUIT YOUR PREFERENCES AND THE CAPABILITIES OF YOUR SYSTEM.

Saved Games

What gets stored when you save your city? A whole bunch of things:

NOTE

IF YOU WANT TO CHANGE THE NAME OF YOUR CITY (SAY IT USED TO BE "DULLSVILLE" AND NOW IT IS "ACTIONTOWN") OR YOU WANT TO CHANGE YOUR MAYORAL NAME, JUST PICK THE "SAVE AS" OPTION AND YOU'LL BE PROMPTED FOR THIS INFORMATION.

- Name of your city
- Your mayoral name
- City statistics, including funds, current date, population, and so on
- Building and Sim status data
- View rotation
- Zoom level
- Business Deals and gifts in toolbar
- Names of any buildings that can be renamed
- Ordinance settings
- Simulation speed—cities always load at PAUSE, but when you start, it resumes at the last speed setting you used
- Landmarks in city and number used, as well as any you can still place
- Auto Budget setting
- Auto Go To setting
- Top-down thumbnail view of the city
- A flag alerting whether you used any cheat codes (useful for contests, school classes, tournaments, and so on)

There are also a number of general *SimCity 3000* settings preferences which are saved as game defaults for all cities:

- Disasters setting
- Sound Effects, Music, and Ambient Sound volume levels
- Tip of the Day setting
- Screen resolution
- Score selection
- System performance settings, including traffic, Sim, and building animations
- Any implicit user-interface settings, such as window positions on the screen

Chapter 5
Starting a Successful City

Many cities will die a premature death if they don't get a good start in life. They stagnate or their treasuries run dry before they can achieve a good tax base. In fact, it's far easier to start an unsuccessful city than to start a thriving one.

In this chapter, we'll give you some guidelines for starting a successful city. Remember, they're just guidelines—tried and true methods for starting out on the right foot.

Terrain

Most people who are building for high density will want a lot of flat land and not too much water. After all, if you're going to try to cram a million or more Sims into your city eventually, you need a lot of space to build. Of course, you can start with any kind of terrain you like, and sometimes the challenge and aesthetics are greater if you don't choose a flat plain.

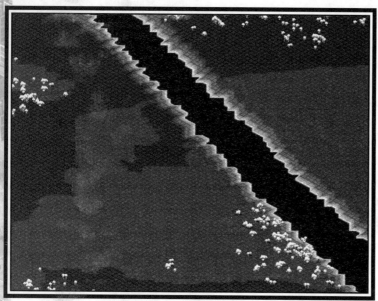

FIG. 5-1. YOU CAN GO FOR A VERY FLAT MAP—SOMETHING EASY TO BUILD ON ...

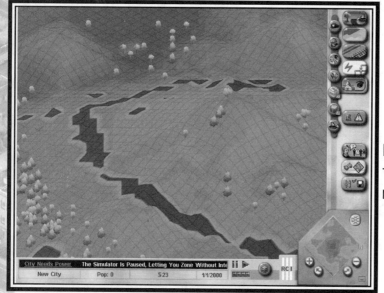

FIG. 5-2. ... OR BUILD SOMETHING MORE IMAGINATIVE ... AND MORE CHALLENGING.

Even if you want to work with predominantly flat land, remember the terrain effects on land value. Elevations higher than average will result in an increase in land value, which is highly desirable. Land built near water also receives a good benefit. So, having some lowlands and some highlands can be very useful. The rule of thumb is to build your industry on the lowlands. Let's face it, dirty industry (the only kind you have if you start your city in 1900) is going to cause land values to be pretty low, so you may as well save your best land for Residential and, to a lesser extent, Commercial zones. For instance, putting a Residential zone on high land, maybe even near some water, will really raise land values so that you might be able to start with high land value, medium-density zones for Residential and start raking in taxes very quickly.

Edge of the Map

It was true in previous versions of *SimCity*, and it's true in this one. If you place polluting and undesirable buildings near the edge of the map, their negative effects on your city will be reduced. So, placing your Coal power plant and your dirty industry near one edge means that nearly half of their pollution output goes off the map and at least some of their NIMBY effects never affect your city.

FIG. 5-3. USE THE EDGE OF THE MAP TO SET YOUR POWER PLANTS AND INDUSTRIAL ZONES.

Keep Industry Separate

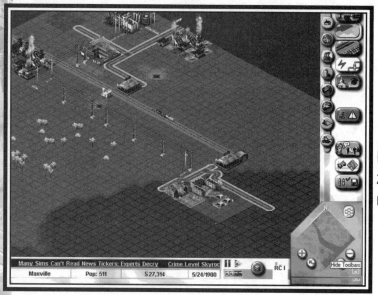

FIG. 5-4. KEEP YOUR OTHER ZONES AWAY FROM ALL THAT DIRTY INDUSTRY.

Industry, because of pollution and NIMBY effects, can really drive down land values. It's best to keep some distance between your Industrial zones and your Residential and Commercial zones. This is particularly important with regard to Residential at the beginning of a city's life span, since Commercial demand will be low to begin with. So, it's a good idea to build Industrial near the edge of the map and on lower terrain, then build your Residential zones some distance away—but not too far. Remember, Sims won't travel endless distances. If a trip is too long, they won't go.

FIG. 5-5. RIGHT FROM THE BEGINNING, YOU CAN USE THE RAILROAD TO ALLOW YOUR SIMS TO TRAVEL FARTHER. DON'T FORGET THAT YOU'LL NEED TRACKS AND A STATION, WHICH SHOULD BE ACCESSIBLE FROM YOUR ZONE.

When you consider the distance the Sims will have to travel, it immediately becomes apparent that mass transit, which allows Sims to travel farther, will be a great benefit. So, consider running roads from your first Residential zones to a train station. Then run your train to your Industrial zone. Some people choose to make the train the only transportation leading to the Industrial zone. Others might back up the train with roads, since Residential Sims will not always take mass transit. Once buses become available, you'll be able to build bus stops along your roads. Buses have some advantages over trains in that Sims can get off anywhere along the route. Combining a good bus network with some railroads can help your Sims move around while keeping traffic congestion to a minimum. At the beginning, providing mass transit will effectively extend the distance you can make between zones.

Train Stations

If you do build a train network, be sure that each of the three zones can be reached from a train station. One way to accomplish this is to have a single train station near (within three to five tiles) all three zones, or simply have a few stations that, between them, cover all three zones.

Make Neighbor Connections

In *SimCity 3000*, your neighbors can be very important to the success of your city. Even though making connections to your neighbors is expensive, especially on your early, limited budget, such connections do serve very important purposes. Building a road or rail connection will increase traffic to your zones. Sims will travel in and out of your city, which means your businesses will have plenty of traffic and demand will continue to rise.

FIG. 5-6. MAKE CONNECTIONS WITH YOUR NEIGHBORS EARLY.

Building a power or water connection to a neighbor can allow you to sell either power or water to that neighbor—or both! You may find that, early on, the money a neighboring city will pay for the excess power from your power plant, or for water you are pumping from your lakes or rivers, can provide a very significant and steady source of income. This income will give you time to keep building your city's infrastructure while your population increases and taxes begin to flow in. If you've used terrain effects wisely and have maximized land values, then your taxes should begin to become lucrative.

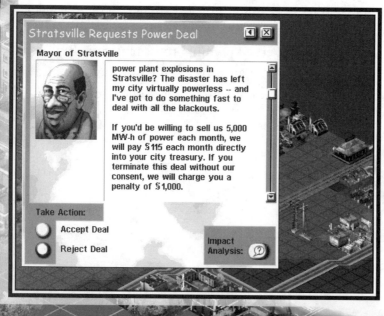

FIG. 5-7. NEIGHBOR DEALS CAN BE GOOD CASH COWS. THEY CAN ALSO SERVE OTHER PURPOSES.

Watch Neighbor Deals and, if they ever stop being a benefit, then don't renew the contract with your neighbor. A deal is a deal, but these deals don't last forever.

You can build multiple connections to the same neighbor. For instance, more road or rail connections to a neighbor means more traffic moving between the cities, which is beneficial early on. Additional water or power connections don't really do much, but they do give you some added security in case of a disaster that breaks one of the existing connections. Because of the cost, you won't be making a lot of redundant connections right off the bat.

Start in a Corner

If you can possibly do so, start your city in or near a corner. Because Neighbor Deals can be so useful, you'll be in a position to make connections with two neighbors very quickly. This can be very helpful if you want your city to grow quickly.

The City Center Effect

FIG. 5-8. THE EFFECTIVE CITY CENTER ALWAYS STARTS WITH THE HIGHEST LAND VALUE.

Planning ahead is generally a good idea. You should take into account the kind of city you want to build and how it should be laid out. This comes with experience, but it will help you realize that there is a special effect in the game, called the "City Center Effect." The City Center Effect means that base land value will be at its highest at the effective center of your city—in fact up to 600 percent higher! This doesn't necessarily mean the center of the map, but rather the center of building and development. The effect extends over a specific range. It doesn't affect Industrial zones because Industrial buildings don't change based on land value. To understand this, we recommend you read the section on the City Center Effect in Chapter 6: Land Development and the RCI Model.

Initial Tax Rates

Keep taxes low at first. When taxes are low, demand is stimulated. Some players even prefer to lower Residential tax rates to zero to encourage lots of Sims to move into the city. This is a good technique because you're going to need to attract Sims in order to collect taxes in the first place. Combined with a lucrative Neighbor Deal, you may find your city growing very quickly.

Zone for Low Density

It's tempting to start out zoning everything for high-density development. After all, high-density land can accommodate all three densities of development. Don't do it. Start with low density. High-density zones are far more expensive to create, and they're actually less likely to develop with the low land values you'll start out with than low-density zones. You can always redevelop the land later, if you can find ways to increase land values. The only exception to this rule is that some Residential zones, if you take full advantage of the terrain effects of water and elevation, may be able to build at medium density right from the start.

Water

For the most part, water is very important if you want your city to grow beyond low density. Although it's technically feasible to build a city without water, it's not advisable. Early on, build a Water Pump, or, if no water is nearby, a Water Tower. Then hook it up to your city using Water Mains in the Pipes View.

Landfills

Be sure to zone a small area as a landfill to take away garbage, and plan to expand it as time goes on. Landfills don't need power or water, but they must have some transportation leading to them.

Industry in Residential

Mostly, you want to keep your Industrial and Residential zones separate. However, if you are worried that your Sims aren't making enough successful trips to work, you can add a few (like maybe 2 × 2) tiles of Industrial zone right next to some Residential. This pretty much guarantees that trips will be successful from that Residential area. However, because you're only placing a very small amount of industry there, the land value effect will be relatively small.

Build Only What You Need

Sometimes there's a tendency to try to build huge zones with a whole grid of transportation before there's enough demand for it. That all costs you money that you might be better off not spending immediately. Moreover, if you build a lot of roads that aren't being used, you'll be paying monthly maintenance costs on those roads; another waste of money.

It's good to build less and let zones grow completely rather than keep adding and adding new areas when the old ones aren't fully developed. Consider plopping some water or a few parks near your zones to increase land value and thereby increase tax revenue and the density of development that the land can support.

Plan for Redevelopment

Don't expect your first zoning and development to be permanent. In *SimCity 3000*, you'll almost certainly have to demolish whole zones and redevelop them as your city grows and new technologies become available. Don't be afraid to build your city with that in mind.

Important Ordinances

Two very important ordinances to pass as soon as possible are the Shuttle Ordinance, which increases the distance that Sims will travel to transportation, and the Subsidize Mass Transit Ordinance, which significantly increases the likelihood that Sims will use mass transit instead of their cars.

Build Larger Grids

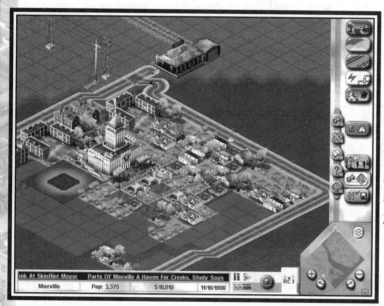

FIG. 5-9. SOMETIMES THE MOST EFFICIENT PLAN ISN'T THE ONLY WAY TO GO. YOU MAY GAIN SOME ADVANTAGES BY USING EXTRA SPACE IN THE MIDDLE OF LARGE ZONES.

If a Sim will travel four tiles to get to a transportation network, you would think that building road grids of 8 × 8 or even 8 × 16 would be most efficient. However, it turns out that some Mayors actually build larger areas—even 12 × 16. The way the distance to transportation is measured, only one edge of a building must be within the allowable distance. Because some buildings are 2 × 2, 3 × 3, or even 4 × 4, you may find that buildings will appear in the extra space you've created. And if nothing builds, you can place parks, water, or police stations to enhance land values in the zone.

Disasters: On or Off?

Disasters in the form of fire, tornado, earthquake, riots, or even alien invasion, can strike at any time. You can turn Disasters off and remain ever safe from such destructive and uncontrollable events, but then you'll miss out on some of the great challenges of *SimCity*, not to mention some of the coolest animations and effects.

If you do choose to leave Disasters on, here are a few tips:

- Build Fire Departments and be prepared to dispatch them to the scene of any fires that break out. You'll have one fire crew for each station you build, plus one extra bucket brigade. In case of fire, use them!
- Watch the news tickers. There are warning signs for some disasters. Items about dogs and cats being nervous or otherwise behaving strangely may mean an earthquake is imminent. Items mentioning unusual weather patterns may mean it's tornado time.
- Worried about earthquakes? Enact the Earthquake Resistance and Retrofitting Ordinance to reduce the amount of damage your city will incur.
- If you do see signs of an upcoming tornado, issue an early warning using the EWS (Early Warning Siren)—if you do, you'll be eligible for more Disaster Relief. To use the EWS, click on the Emergency button, then click on Activate Warning Siren. Don't overuse it, though. If you sound a false alarm too often, your Sims will stop believing you and the EWS will be ineffective.
- Aliens will always go after landmarks first, but if there are no landmarks, they'll attack your most expensive structures like power plants, Airports, etc. Solution? Place a landmark or two in your city.

Use the Query Tool

FIG. 5-10. GET USED TO THE QUERY TOOL. IT'S A MICROSCOPE INTO YOUR CITY.

The Query tool is very useful. Click it on just about anything in the game and you'll get information about that object. When you're getting started, keep looking at your land and buildings to see their status. You can learn about whether they're powered and watered, how much power and water they consume, what the land value is worth, and much more, depending on the building or object queried.

Advisors and Petitioners

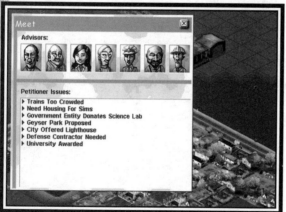

FIG. 5-11. KEEP AN OPEN DOOR POLICY WITH YOUR ADVISORS AND ALSO WITH ANY PETITIONERS WHO MAY WANT TO SPEAK WITH YOU.

When severely in doubt, check with your city advisors. You never know. They might have some good advice. Also, check messages from Petitioners. You may not find all their suggestions, demands, and gripes useful in every case, but they do present some good information from time to time, and they often offer good deals worth taking.

Time to get started. What are you waiting for?

Chapter 6
Land Development and the RCI Model

Succeeding at *SimCity 3000* is largely a matter of making good decisions and taking appropriate actions. To make the best decisions, it's good to take a look at what's happening in your city. You're the mayor of a dynamic and almost-living city, and there are a lot of forces influencing it. In a sense, though you are constantly making decisions about your city, its actual development is only indirectly affected by your actions. Why? What's going on behind the scenes that determines how your city will grow?

The first and most important aspect of your city's inner workings is the concept of how land development takes place.

This chapter deals with the basics of land development in *SimCity 3000* by examining:

- Basic SimEconomics: RCI Supply and Demand
- Other RCI Factors
- Zone Types
- Land Value Determination
- Development Logic and General Building Rules

Basic SimEconomics: RCI Supply and Demand

One basis of *SimCity* is the concept of supply and demand—Economics 101. Various kinds of supply and demand effects concern your city:

FIG. 6-1. CITY DEVELOPMENT TAKES PLACE PRIMARILY IN THE THREE ZONE TYPES: RESIDENTIAL, COMMERCIAL, AND INDUSTRIAL.

Industrial Supply and Demand

In an Industrial zone, buildings are constructed if there's demand for industry. This demand is initially generated from outside your city, which is why your city always starts off with some demand for industry. Later, as your city's population grows, internal Industrial demand is generated, adding to the external demand. As Industrial buildings are constructed, each building decreases Industrial demand in proportion to its density. When Industrial buildings are constructed, they create a need for workers, which translates into Residential demand because the workers need somewhere to live. Industrial connections relieve Industrial growth caps. The same thing is true of ports. So, as Industrial demand increases and more Industrial zones are populated with buildings, Residential demand also increases.

Commercial Supply and Demand

Both internal and external forces stimulate Commercial demand. It's assumed that there's some need for Commercial services from outside the city—banking and tourism, primarily—but most Commercial demand will be generated by the people of your city; in other words, by your Residential population. Therefore, Commercial demand is largely a function of population. Commercial buildings also need workers, so the construction of buildings in a Commercial zone also increases Residential demand. Each Commercial building constructed reduces Commercial demand according to its density. If you think of the density of a Commercial building as a function of how many jobs it creates, it's clear that, as with Industry, more jobs create a demand for more housing and, therefore, greater Residential demand.

Residential Supply and Demand

Residential demand measures the demand for workers to fill the jobs generated by Industrial and Commercial activity. The basic formula for calculating Residential demand is to add Industrial and Commercial. Stated as a formula, it is:

$$R = C + I$$

As your Industrial and Commercial zones grow, demand for new housing in the form of Residential zoning will increase. If your city falls on hard times and Industrial and Commercial buildings are being abandoned, demand for Residential buildings will decrease, possibly resulting in the abandonment of previously constructed Residential areas. Each Residential building decreases Residential demand according to its density. In other words, as houses and apartment blocks are constructed, there are fewer Sims out there milling around, looking for good neighborhoods in which to live.

RCI values range from -2,000 to 2,000, so the maximum demand possible is 2,000. Anything below zero is negative demand.

Negative Demand

Negative demand occurs when the system is out of balance, and can cause already-developed buildings in affected zones to be abandoned. For instance, if Industrial or Commercial zones are highly developed, but there aren't enough people to fill the jobs, a negative demand situation results. A factory that can't hire enough workers to run the assembly line obviously can't make its deliveries; being unable to turn a profit, any such company will soon close its doors and go out of business. Of course, this situation may be balanced by increased Residential demand. Conversely, if there aren't enough jobs for the existing population, a negative Residential demand is created and some Sims may go off in search of greener pastures.

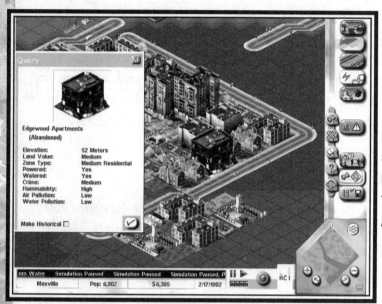

FIG. 6-2. WHEN NEGATIVE DEMAND IS CREATED, YOU MAY SEE SOME OF YOUR BUILDINGS BEING ABANDONED, ALTHOUGH THERE MAY BE OTHER FACTORS AT WORK.

Demand Cycles and Ratios

SimCity 3000 begins with relatively high Industrial demand. As Industrial buildings spring up, Residential demand follows accordingly. However, as a city grows, its economy tends to become more internal—meaning that Commercial demand begins to catch up with, and ultimately surpass, Industrial demand. When a city is first established, Industrial demand is roughly five times that of Commercial demand, or a ratio of 5:1. As a city approaches a population of 233,000, that ratio gradually changes to 1:1. Above 233,000, the ratio begins to favor Commercial, until it reaches a maximum of approximately 1:4 or 80 percent Commercial to 20 percent Industrial.

Practically speaking, what does this mean? When you begin to zone your city, you'll want to create Industrial zones first, then Residential, then Commercial. You should follow the **R = C + I** rule and create approximately equal Residential zoning to the sum of Industrial and Commercial, although you may find that Residential demand tends to lead the way at times.

Suppose you were to create an Industrial zone of 15 tiles. According to this formula, you would create a Residential zone of 20 tiles and a Commercial zone of 5 tiles ($R = C + I$). Practically speaking, these figures are only a rule of thumb. You'll want to watch the RCI graph at the bottom of the screen for clues. Also, watch how fast your zones develop, and at what density and land value. And, of course, there are many factors that affect land development in addition to the simple supply and demand model expressed here.

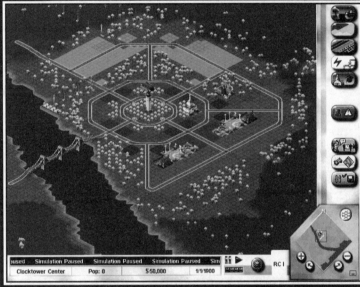

FIG. 6-3. YOU WANT TO BALANCE RESIDENTIAL ZONING AGAINST THE SUM OF COMMERCIAL AND INDUSTRIAL.

Other RCI Factors

In addition to the very basic supply and demand model, some other factors directly affect the RCI in your city. These factors include the specific zoning and buildings that have developed, taxation, ordinances, and certain RCI caps built into the simulation.

Specific Zone Development

Land uses in specific zones directly affect RCI supply and demand as seen in Table 6-1, which shows the specific per tile effect of buildings in different zone types and densities in terms of 1×1 buildings. A 2×2 building would supply four times the number listed. A 3 × 3 building has nine times the effect. And so forth.

All developed tiles and filler can affect RCI supply and demand, though abandoned and construction states have no effect.

TABLE 6-1. EFFECTS OF ZONE DEVELOPMENT ON RCI SUPPLY AND DEMAND

Zone	Supplies Residential	Demands Workers	Supplies Commercial	Supplies Industrial
LD, LV Res	20			
LD, MV Res	20			
LD, HV Res	20			
MD, LV Res	40			
MD, MV Res	40			
MD, HV Res	40			
HD, LV Res	80			
HD, MV Res	80			
HD, HV Res	80			
LD Dirty Ind		10		10
LD Clean Ind		10		10
LD Agriculture		1		1
MD Dirty Ind		20		20
MD Clean Ind		20		20
HD Dirty Ind		40		40
HD Clean Ind		40		40
LD LMV Com		10	10	
LD MHV Com		10	10	
MD LMV Com		20	20	
MD MHV Com		20	20	
HD LMV Com		40	40	
HD MHV Com		40	40	

As you can see from Table 6-1, Residential development of any density provides twice the Residential supply as its equivalent in either Commercial or Industrial. For instance, low-density Residential development supplies 20 workers per tile while low-density Commercial and Industrial each create a demand of 10.

Some special buildings can affect RCI supply and demand as well. For instance, a police station increases Residential demand because it requires workers. A MegaMall supplies a great deal of Commercial, thereby significantly reducing Commercial demand. It also requires workers, so it can increase Residential demand a little.

Taxation

Unless you work for a tax agency, you probably cringe a little when you hear the word "taxes." Not to worry. This time, you are the government, and taxes are your friend. Yes, the shoe's on the other foot now, and you'll want to milk, squeeze, and extract every spare Simolean from your city's businesses and residents. This is all for their own good, of course, because how else can you provide them with the wonderful city services that they demand?

Taxes are your main tool for generating city income. Also, through the careful tuning of your tax rates, you can have a significant effect on RCI supply and demand. Each sector—Residential, Commercial, and Industrial—has its own tax rate that you can adjust separately. In this way, you have some control over revenue and demand in each sector.

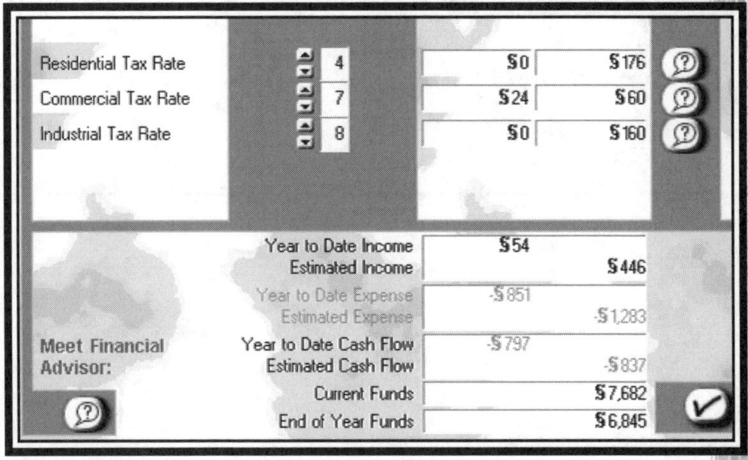

FIG. 6-4. SET THE TAX RATES YOU
WANT FOR EACH ZONE TYPE.

Low taxes can create an increased demand for a specific zone type, while high taxes cause a negative effect. When a city is small, Sim sensitivity to tax rates is at its minimum. This means that Sims will tolerate somewhat higher taxes with little or no effect on demand; additionally, lower taxes will have a greater positive effect on demand when a city's population is small. As the city grows, sensitivity to higher taxes becomes greater and the positive effect of lower taxes is reduced. Table 6-2 shows the basic effect of tax rates on demand with increases in population. The first column displays the city's population. The second number indicates the tax rate at which there is no effect on demand. Any tax rate below that will increase demand while any tax rate above that rate will reduce demand. Looking at the table, you can see that at population zero, taxes below nine percent tend to add demand while taxes above nine percent cause a negative effect. In other words, a nine percent tax rate is neutral and has no effect on demand one way or the other. Also, the positive effect on demand at zero tax rate and zero population represents a 30 percent increase. Contrast that with a city population of 250,000 where taxes below five percent create positive demand, but even at a tax rate of zero, the demand is only increased by five percent. Negative demand effects at maximum tax rates (up to 22 percent) are far heavier and range from -75 percent to -140 percent. Commercial, Industrial, and Residential taxpayers are all assumed to have the same levels of sensitivity to tax rates.

TABLE 6-2. POPULATION EFFECTS ON TAX SENSITIVITY

Population	No Effect	0% Tax	22% Tax
0	9% tax	+30%	-70%
50,000	7% tax	+15%	-90%
100,000	7% tax	+10%	-100%
200,000	6% tax	+8%	-130%
250,000	5% tax	+5%	-140%

From zero population and up to 50,000, taxes above nine percent create a negative effect on demand, but does that mean that you should never use taxes above nine percent? Certainly not! If demand is high enough, the negative modifier won't decrease it enough to prevent growth, and the additional income may be critical to improving conditions in the city—thereby further increasing demand. Remember that many other factors figure into RCI demand, including specific ordinances and city services like police, fire, hospitals, schools, and recreation. These services affect land values, which in turn affect both demand and density.

Tax Revenues

Tax revenues are a function of population and average land value. The formula for calculating tax revenue is:

$$\textbf{revenue} = \textbf{tax rate} \times \textbf{supply} \times \textbf{average LV} \times \textbf{TaxTransmogrifier}$$

In the formula, supply is based on population, *average LV* is the city's average land value, and the *TaxTransmogrifier* is a special number used to modify the revenue. There's a different TaxTransmogrifier number for each zone type.

Obviously, keeping land values high will result in more revenues. One of the keys to success in *SimCity 3000* is to maximize the value of your city's zones. More on land values later … .

Ordinances, Neighbor Deals, Business Deals, and loans all can have a direct impact on the city budget. For these budget items, the effect—plus or minus—is calculated separately from the tax table demand adjustment. So, with effective use of taxation and ordinances, you can have a moderate amount of control over your city's growth.

Tax Loss Incentives

Sometimes you'll want to reduce taxes to a losing percentage to stimulate demand in one of the zones. For instance, some old-time SimCity mayors like to set Residential tax rates at zero when they first start building their cities. You don't lose any significant income, since there's nobody to pay taxes anyway, and you rapidly stimulate Residential demand, which in turn builds your population more quickly. Then, when you raise taxes, say to six or eight percent, you have a larger tax base already in place.

At any time when RCI demand begins to drop, you have the option to lower taxes in the particular affected zones, thereby stimulating the economy. Juggling income versus economic stimulation is one of the constant tasks you'll encounter as you watch over your city. However, remember that Table 6-2 shows how the effect of such juggling is more favorable when the city's population is small and becomes less so as population increases.

TIP

THE WAY THE SIMULATION WORKS, EVEN LAND WITH THE LOWEST VALUE WILL PRODUCE SOME TAXES. THIS IS A GREAT BENEFIT AT THE BEGINNING OF A CITY'S DEVELOPMENT, THOUGH IT WILL HAVE LITTLE EFFECT LATER ON. WHAT IT MEANS IS THAT WHEN YOUR CITY FIRST STARTS OUT, EVEN THE SCUMMIEST ZONE ON YOUR MAP WILL PRODUCE TAX REVENUE FOR YOU. AND TAX REVENUE IS SOMETHING YOU'LL NEED PLENTY OF.

RCI Caps

Demand for Residential (R), Commerical (C), or Industrial (I) may reach certain milestones, or caps, that require some action on your part. In the case of Residential demand, citizens may demand some form of recreation like a Marina, Stadium, or Zoo. Commercial and Industrial caps can be alleviated by building or expanding Airports and Seaports, or by establishing additional road/rail connections to neighbors.

The concept of cap relief being per cell is slightly abstract; let's use "per building" in the hopes that it's easier to grasp. Table 6-4 shows the effect that certain solutions have on various demand caps. Caps relief is measured per unit, i.e., 25,000 caps relief will supply 25,000 Residential/Industrial/Commercial caps relief. Values listed are per tile, so, for instance, a Museum, which occupies a 3 × 3 area provides 1,000 times 16 or 9,000 additional Residential relief.

FIG. 6-5. PLACING RECREATIONAL BUILDINGS IN YOUR CITY IS NECESSARY TO HELP IT GROW.

Despite all other factors, population will never reach the 100,000 cap unless you have enough of the recreational buildings to provide the necessary cap relief. This could be eleven museums (9,000x11), seven zoos (24,000 x 7), etc. It is a good idea to place reward buildings as you receive them from your petitioners. Each of these provides caps relief.

Table 6-4. Caps Relief Solutions and Values

Structure	R Cap	C Cap	I Cap
Library	7,000		
Performing Arts Center	48,000	—	—
Museum	9,000	—	—
Geyser Park	25,000	—	—
Lighthouse	6,000	—	—
Marina	9,000	—	—
City Zoo	24,000	—	—
Stadium	125,000	—	—
Country Club	37,500	—	—
Theme Park	200,000	—	—
Small Park	250	—	—
Big Park	2,250	—	—
Baseball Field	4,000	—	—
Playground	1,000	—	—
Pond	1,000	—	—
Fountain	250	—	—
Mayor's House	6,000	—	—
City Hall	9,000	—	—
Historic Statue	10,000	—	—
County Courthouse	9,000	—	—
Casino Row	75,000	—	—
Gigamall	25,000	—	—
Airport (per tile)	—	500	100
Seaport (per tile)	—	100	250
*Spaceport	750,000	750,000	750,000
Highway Connection	—	20,000	14,000
Rail Connection	—	—	25,000
Road Connection	—	12,000	12,000
Subway Connection	—	25,000	—

*the ultimate cap reliever.

Zone Development

Understanding how supply and demand work in *SimCity 3000* is an essential element of the decision-making process. But, the main tool for implementing that knowledge is zoning. You can create the following types of zones:

Low-density Residential: supports only low-density Residential buildings

Medium-density Residential: supports low- and medium-density buildings

High-density Residential: supports low-, medium-, and high-density buildings

Low-density Commercial: supports only low-density Commercial buildings

Medium-density Commercial: supports low- and medium-density Commercial buildings

High-density Commercial: supports low-, medium-, and high-density Commercial buildings

Low-density Industrial: supports only low-density Industrial buildings and agriculture

Medium-density Industrial: supports low- and medium-density Industrial buildings

High-density Industrial: supports low-, medium-, and high-density Industrial buildings

Airport: "puzzle zone" (see page 27) that builds an Airport only if the minimum size (3 × 5 tiles) is available, and all contiguous tiles are flat

Seaport: puzzle zone that builds a Seaport if located next to navigable water

Landfill: puzzle zone that creates a landfill to process garbage (must be 2x2 to be used)

Unzoned: includes roads and networks, trees, and plopped buildings such as landmarks, civic buildings, and other special buildings

Fig. 6-6. Zones of different densities will affect what buildings can be constructed.

Zone Density

"All right," you may be saying to yourself. "I just ought to zone everything as 'high density,' because that's what allows for low-, medium-, and high-density development." Seems straightforward, no? Well, actually—no. First of all, it's very expensive to zone land for high-density development. It's literally *five times as costly* to zone high density versus low.

TABLE 6-5. RELATIVE COSTS OF ZONE DENSITY PLACEMENT

Zone Density	Cost
Low	§10/tile
Medium	§20/tile
High	§50/tile

Therefore, it becomes clear that, early in the game, it's incredibly easy to bust your budget if you try to start off using high-density zoning. What's more, land zoned for high density may have some trouble getting low-density development because of low or fluctuating land values.

Second, there's an additional element of strategy integral to *SimCity 3000*: urban renewal. Your Sims are practically *expecting* you to bring in the bulldozers every now and then to knock down old eyesores, rezone the area to higher density or different use, and allow the SimArchitects the chance to put up brand new buildings. This enhances

your city's aesthetics, too, because unlike in *SimCity 2000*, each zone density has unique buildings that will develop depending on land values. Variety is the spice of life, and you get plenty of it when you rezone with new densities and at new land values.

FIG. 6-7. YOU SHOULD EXPECT SOME URBAN RENEWAL IN YOUR CITY'S LONG-RANGE PLAN.

Finally, a city isn't a static thing, like a house of cards, where you carefully add here and there, but never touch the essential structure. In *SimCity 3000*, the emphasis is on the *dynamic*—your city is expected to undergo fairly radical changes in layout and structure as it evolves.

So, don't be afraid to zone for low-density development. Your city layout is going to change over time anyway, so it's generally not worth it to try to set up everything as if it's going to remain static forever.

City Zone and Density Maps

To get a graphical look at your city's zoning and population density, open the City Map and choose Zones and Density. The Zones map shows the following zone types, each in a different color:

Residential
Commercial
Industrial
Government
Airports
Seaports
Landfill

Unzoned areas are displayed in gray.

The Density map simply shows a gradient of color representing the population density as it's distributed over the City Map.

FIG. 6-8. USE THE ZONE DENSITY MAP TO GET A QUICK OVERVIEW OF YOUR ZONE DEVELOPMENT.

Determining Land Values

Land value is the single most important factor considered before construction begins on a new building. Land value itself is affected by several factors:

- Proximity to City Center
- Air pollution
- Water pollution
- Accumulated garbage
- Radiation
- Crime
- NIMBY/YIMBY factors
- Terrain effects

Pollution and Crime

Pollution and crime can affect land value. No surprise there. However, the way land value is calculated needs some explanation. There's an arbitrary value set within the simulation that states what the "average" pollution or crime level is. Any value above that is considered to be above average and will lower land value by a certain percentage, based on the actual amount of pollution or crime. Similarly, if pollution or crime are below average, the land value of affected tiles will be higher.

Pollution effects are strictly additive, so clustering polluting buildings together is not a bad idea.

TIP

IT WAS TRUE IN SIMCITY 2000, AND IT'S STILL TRUE NOW. IF YOU CLUSTER YOUR WORST POLLUTERS—POWER PLANTS, DIRTY INDUSTRY, INCINERATORS, ETC.—ON THE EDGE OF YOUR MAP, EFFECTIVELY HALF OF THEIR POLLUTION EFFECT WILL GO AWAY, PRESUMABLY TO YOUR NEIGHBOR CITIES, BUT THAT'S NOT YOUR PROBLEM. IT'S HIGHLY RECOMMENDED THAT YOU PLACE YOUR WORST POLLUTERS AT THE MAP EDGE AND AWAY FROM YOUR RESIDENTIAL AND COMMERCIAL ZONES.

Garbage

Garbage, if not properly disposed of, accumulates on filler tiles in various zones. The amount of garbage that accumulates directly affects the land values, and if garbage is visible on filler tiles, it's also assumed to be present on tiles with buildings as well. Although it will take about a year for the effects of accumulated garbage to be seen in building downgrades and abandonment, the effect on land value is immediate. Moreover, the more garbage that builds up, the more it affects land value.

NIMBY/YIMBY

Almost every building in *SimCity 3000* has some effect on neighboring tiles. This effect is often referred to as NIMBY (Not In My Back Yard) or YIMBY (Yes In My Back Yard). NIMBY is a negative effect, which lowers land values, causing less upscale or lower-density buildings to be constructed. YIMBY is a positive effect, which raises land values and has the opposite effect on building results.

Some buildings have very strong NIMBY effects; for instance, nobody particularly wants to live next to a prison or a toxic waste dump, so these buildings have strong NIMBY effects on the surrounding areas. On the other hand, some structures, such as parks, trees, schools, and police stations, have positive (YIMBY) effects. Other buildings have mixed effects—NIMBY for one kind of zone and YIMBY for another. An example is a bus station, which has a slightly NIMBY effect on Residential zones (people don't like living right next to where noisy, diesel-spewing buses stop and go at all hours of the day and night), but a YIMBY effect on Commercial and Industrial areas (because the buses bring Sims to shop and work there). Unlike pollution, which actually radiates from a building to the surrounding tiles, NIMBY and YIMBY effects only raise or lower local average land values, causing land values to change in the general area according to how strong the NIMBY or YIMBY effect is. The effect is expressed as a positive or negative number, which is translated into a percentage of the land value of the surrounding tiles. If the number is positive, this percentage is added to the current land value for a YIMBY effect. If it's negative, this percentage is subtracted from surrounding land values for a NIMBY effect.

A practical example: You create a Residential zone and watch it build, then place a Coal power plant right next to that Residential zone. A Coal power plant has a pretty strong NIMBY effect (not to mention the air and water pollution it emits), so previously existing buildings near the plant will tend to be abandoned and eventually replaced with buildings of much lower value. The land value next to the Coal plant has been reduced by 28 percent by the NIMBY factor alone. On the other hand, move the Coal plant away from the Residential zone and place some parks, fountains, and gazebos near it, and you'll get a YIMBY effect that raises land values and allows a better quality of buildings to be created. (Add a nearby police station and you'll get lower crime than the average, which again raises land value.)

FIG. 6-9. NIMBY EFFECTS, ESPECIALLY WHEN COMBINED WITH POLLUTION, CAN SEVERELY LOWER LAND VALUES AND CAUSE ZONES TO DEGRADE.

For information about NIMBY and YIMBY effects of specific buildings, see Appendix A.

Terrain Effects

Land value is affected by certain terrain effects—specifically elevation and proximity to water. Land values are greater near water and also for tiles that are higher than the average city elevation. Land on top of a hill receives a boost in land value that is proportionate to its elevation above the map average. This effect can be quite significant because it changes the Base Land Value, from which all other land values are calculated. Most factors affect the final, calculated land value, but terrain effects work directly on the base value and therefore can cause far more significant changes to land value. The terrain effect of building near water extends for about six or seven tiles, diminishing with distance. So, if you want to get maximum land values, it's a good idea to build Residential zones near water or around hills to benefit from the land value increase.

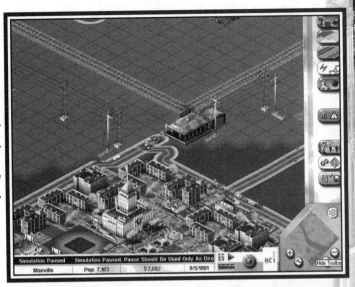

FIG. 6-10. THE TERRAIN EFFECT CAN PROVIDE A SIGNIFICANT DIFFERENCE IN LAND VALUE AND, ULTIMATELY, TAX REVENUE.

TIP

WANT A QUICK LAND VALUE BOOST? EASY. FOLLOW ALL THE GUIDELINES IN THIS CHAPTER. OH, AND TRY ADDING SOME WATER FEATURES. YES, YOU CAN BUILD A LITTLE POND AND BENEFIT FROM THE TERRAIN EFFECT. THIS GIVES YOU SOME ADDED CONTROL ON LAND VALUE BECAUSE YOU COULD, FOR INSTANCE, PLOP A LITTLE WATER IN THE MIDDLE OF A RESIDENTIAL ZONE AND ITS EFFECT ON SURROUNDING TILES WOULD RAISE LAND VALUE. ALSO, BECAUSE WATER WILL ADD ZERO TO LOCAL POLLUTION AND CRIME, IT TENDS TO DRIVE DOWN THE AVERAGE OF THESE EFFECTS, FURTHER INCREASING LAND VALUE. (THIS IS TRUE OF ANYTHING YOU PUT INTO YOUR ZONES THAT DOESN'T HAVE CRIME OR POLLUTION ASSOCIATED WITH IT. BECAUSE OF THE ACCUMULATION OF POLLUTION AND CRIME EFFECTS AND THEIR ULTIMATE IMPACT ON LOCAL LAND VALUE, ADDING SOMETHING THAT LOWERS THE LOCAL AVERAGE TENDS TO HAVE A POSITIVE EFFECT.)

The City Center Effect on Land Value

The City Center is the center of zoned and built areas as opposed to the geographical center. Land value is highest at the City Center and decreases from that point to the edge of the developed city. The designers of SC3000 based this concept on the idea that the center "downtown" of a city should have higher land value than land farther away. You can still increase the land value of outlying areas with Parks, proximity to water, other YIMBY buildings, etc.

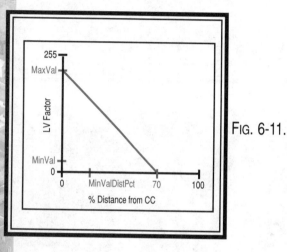

FIG. 6-11.

Figure 6-11 shows that base land value is 255 (MaxVal) at the City Center. Land value drops off linearly until it reaches a specific distance away from City Center. From that point to the edge of the city terrain, the land value remains constant at the lowest value (MinVal). MinVal is a specific value that is set within the simulation for each zone type. If land values were §500,000 at the city center, they would fall linearly to that set value at the point determined to be the MinVDP% (MinValDistPct in figure 6-11), or minimum value distance percentage. This point is also determined specifically in the simulation for each zone type and is expressed as a percentage of the distance from the City Center to the edge of the map.

As an example, suppose the MaxVal of Residential land is §500,000, which, discounting other factors, is what it is at the City Center. Now let's suppose that the simulation sets MinVal at §7,500 and MinVDP% at 70. What this means is that Residential land values will fall on a linear scale from zero percent to 70 percent of the distance from the City Center until they reach §7,500 at the 70 percent point. From there to the edge of the map, (once again discounting other factors), Residential land value will be §7,500. These figures may be different for Commercial and Industrial land values. Note that this example doesn't reflect actual figures from the game.

FIG. 6-12. THE HIGH-VALUE LAND AT THE CITY CENTER IS THE ONLY PLACE WHERE THE LARGEST 4 × 4 COMMERCIAL BUILDINGS CAN BE BUILT.

Note that the City Center effect is calculated based on Base Land Value. Like terrain effects, this effect is very strong because it modifies land value before other modifiers are calculated. Also note that, as you build your city, the effective City Center will change. There are techniques for designing a city to maximize and control this effect, but if you build haphazardly, you'll see some fluctuations in land values based on the movement of the City Center.

How is the City Center Calculated?

Quoting from the *SimCity 3000* design documents:

    City Center is calculated by taking the average of the centers of all the buildings in the city. The effect of city center is based on the distance, which uses a modified Manhattan distance calculation (as shown in figure 6-13):

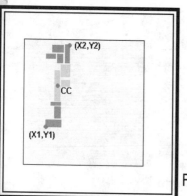

If (Y2 - Y1 < X2 - X1) then
MMD = X2 - X1 + (Y2 - Y1)/2
else
MMD = Y2 - Y1 + (X2 - X1)/2

FIG. 6-13.

Summary of Land Value Effects

Land value is one of the more complex calculations that happen in *SimCity 3000*. Land value is reassessed approximately every 60 days. It's determined by the factors discussed previously—pollution, crime, NIMBY/YIMBY effects, terrain effects, and distance from the calculated City Center. The formula used to determine land value would read something like this (minus appropriate modifiers):

LV = (Base Land Value × (City Center + Terrain Effects)) × (Pollution + Crime + NIMBY/YIMBY)

    Remember that pollution and crime can have positive effects on land value if they're lower than average. However, what's important here isn't the formula, but the effects of land value on your mayoral life. There are two fundamental concepts you need to grasp from all these details: Higher land value means more tax revenue, and land value is what determines land use. In other words, the value of the land determines what kind of building will be placed on it. The higher the value, the better the quality and density of building that can be built, and, ultimately, the more taxes you'll collect. The following section expands on this concept.

Development Logic and General Building Rules

Various factors affect whether any particular zoned tile will be developed. The simulation assesses these conditions once each month. Among those factors are:

- Is demand positive?
- Is the tile powered?
- Is the tile within x tiles of transportation (number of tiles varies from zone to zone)?
- Is the tile free of radiation pollution?
- Given land values and space requirements, can anything be built?

If the answer to any of these questions is no, then no development will take place.

Once the determination is made to build on a particular tile or set of tiles, construction will begin after a certain time period, depending on the size of the structure. At this point, several other factors affect what will be built:

- What's the tile's land value (see below)?
- Does the tile have water (see below)?
- For Industrial zones: global EQ (Education Quotient), current ordinances and pollution levels (see section on Industrial Zone Specifics)
- For Industrial zones: land value and distance from city buildings to determine whether agriculture develops
- Certain random criteria and geometry are considered

Buildings will be constructed where possible, and the simulation will also place what are called "filler tiles," which can be such items as lawns, swimming pools, and parking lots.

If the current land value is either too high or too low to match any acceptable land use options, then no development will take place. Table 6-6 lists the range of land use values acceptable to the simulation for each land density type. The simulator will attempt to build a building of the highest possible value for that zone type.

TABLE 6-6. LAND VALUE DEVELOPMENT THRESHOLDS

Residential Density	Low Value	Medium Value	High Value
Low	2,500–187,500	190,000–375,000	377,500–637,500
Medium	2,500–190,000	192,500–425,000	427,500–637,500
High	87,500–217,500	220,000–450,000	452,500–637,500

Commercial Density	Low–Medium Value	Medium–High Value
Low	2,500–222,500	225,000–637,500
Medium	2,500–322,500	325,000–637,500
High	150,000–450,000	452,500–637,500

Industrial Density	Dirty	Clean	Agricultural
Low	2,500–312,500	2,500–437,500	2,500–225,000
Medium	2,500–437,500	2,500–562,500	—
High	2,500–562,500	2,500–637,500	—

Water and Development

Without water, zones won't develop past low density, and puzzle zones such as Airports and Seaports will not develop at all. The following list details what will develop in each zone type without water:

- Residential: low density, low value; low density, medium value only
- Commercial: low density, low value only
- Industrial: low-density dirty or low-density clean only
- "Puzzle zones" (Airports, Seaports, etc.): No development

Distance from Transportation

For any given tile to be built, it must be within a certain distance from transportation. Sims will only walk so far. This distance varies from one zone type to another. Note that only one tile in a building must be within the appropriate distance—not the whole building. Therefore, a 3 × 3 building must only have one edge within the allowable distance. The rest of the building can be farther away.

Still, since SimArchitects and construction workers don't consult with you regarding the exact placement of any given building, it's generally a good idea to build your zone-transportation grid so that all tiles within zones are within the necessary travel distance.

By zone, the distance from transportation that building can take place is:

- Residential: four tiles
- Commercial: three tiles
- Industrial: five tiles
- Agriculture: any part of the development must be within five tiles; however, an individual farm can range between 8 × 8 and 8 × 18. Of course, many individual farms can appear contiguously, so, in actuality, farmland can stretch out to the edges of the map if the proper conditions exist.

NOTE

IN SimCity 2000, EACH ZONE REQUIRED THE SAME THREE TILE DISTANCES TO TRANSPORTATION, WHICH MADE DESIGNING CITIES OFTEN A MATTER OF CREATING GRIDS THAT WERE SIX TILES WIDE, WITH TRANSPORTATION ON EITHER SIDE. THIS STRATEGY WON'T BE THE MOST EFFICIENT IN SimCity 3000.

TIP

THE SHUTTLE ORDINANCE CAUSES ALL TRANSPORTATION DISTANCES TO INCREASE BY ONE, MEANING THAT RESIDENTIAL BECOMES FIVE, COMMERCIAL BECOMES FOUR, AND INDUSTRIAL BECOMES SIX. THE SHUTTLE ORDINANCE IS ALWAYS AVAILABLE. HOWEVER, FOR THE SHUTTLE ORDINANCE TO TAKE EFFECT, YOU MUST HAVE TRAIN, BUS, OR SUBWAY SERVICE IN YOUR CITY.

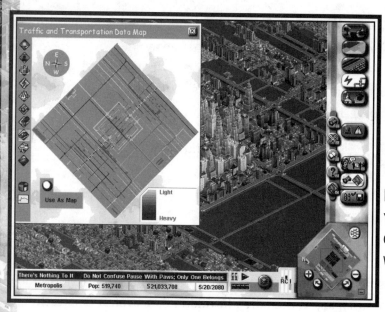

FIG. 6-14. WHEN YOU CREATE YOUR TRANSPORTATION GRID, CONSIDER THE DISTANCES SIMS WILL TRAVEL.

Building Efficient Transportation Grids

The main factors to consider when designing your city are separating polluting buildings from your Residential and Commercial zones, and factoring in the distance Sims will travel to reach transportation. Does this mean that you should get out your slide rule and calculate the absolute perfect, symmetrical layout that will pack the most people into your city? Sure, if that's what you want.

But there are some other ways to approach it. One way is to build grids that are somewhat larger than you might think. For instance, consider that, after enacting the Shuttle Ordinance, your Residential Sims will go five tiles to reach transportation. So, logically, a road surrounding a 10 × 10 tile area would seem to be a pretty good grid to build. Or, perhaps simply two parallel roads separated by 10 tiles and with a cross street every 20 tiles or so might seem like a good idea.

It turns out that there are good reasons for building a slightly larger grid. First, buildings only need to have one edge within the allowable transportation distance. That means that a larger building can partially be built outside that parameter. Moreover, if buildings don't develop, you can place water, parks, and police stations, thereby increasing land value in several ways. For one thing, parks and police stations have YIMBY effects. Parks reduce effective pollution by adding a zero to the averaging of local pollution, which actually has a significant effect. Water will do the same while also producing a positive terrain effect that stretches over several tiles.

Police stations lower crime, and if the crime falls below the city average, which it should, then you get a land value boost. Also, a police station doesn't have to be near transportation, so it can be built in the middle of a zone.

Bottom line? There's more than one way to grid a city, and sometimes the obvious method isn't necessarily the best way.

Construction and Reconstruction

The simulation checks once a month to see if a building can be upgraded, or if it should be downgraded or abandoned.

Construction

When a building is under construction, it's placed in the "construction state." The time of construction is proportional to the size of the building; i.e. a 1 × 1 building takes about one month. A 3 × 3 building takes about three months.

Upgrades

When the simulation determines that a building can be upgraded, there is approximately a 30 percent chance that this will occur. The two primary factors that lead to upgrading are high demand and land value. The simulation uses the normal developer rules to determine what, if any, upgrade should occur. It then places any relevant tiles, including filler tiles if necessary, in the construction state. After the appropriate amount of time has passed, the new building will be displayed.

Construction and Reconstruction

You can mark and unmark a building as historic. If you do so, that building is then impervious to building upgrades. It may still be abandoned, be destroyed by a disaster, or be covered in trash, but it will never be upgraded so long as it's marked historic.

If a historic building is destroyed by a disaster, it loses its historic status.

Also, you can't simply demolish a historic building. To demolish a historic building, you must first uncheck the historic marker in the query window, then demolish the building.

Downgrades

When the simulation determines that a land value in an area has degraded suffi-ciently, a building can "downgrade". For each month that such conditions continue, there is approximately a 20 percent chance that a downgrade will occur. When this happens, the building will change its appearance to a shabbier, more run-down structure, in keeping with its decline in value.

Abandonment

FIG. 6-15.

There is a chance that an existing building may become abandoned if certain con-ditions exist:

- Demand for the zone type is negative along with a random factor calculation based on the current value for demand.
- The building is no longer receiving power (35 percent chance of abandonment).
- The building is no longer receiving water, and land use is above the minimum value or density for unwatered zones (35 percent chance of abandonment).

- The building is no longer within the minimum distance from transportation.
- A trip can't be completed successfully from the building to another zone.
- The building is in an area that has become contaminated by radiation.
- The building has experienced a drastic reduction in land value—for instance, the placement of a large NIMBY feature in a medium- or high-value zone.

An abandoned building may be redeveloped if:

- The conditions that caused the abandonment go away, and the ideal land use for the building is the same as it was previously. In this case, the building reverts to its occupied state.
- If development is possible, the building will switch to a construction state and *Sim City 3000* will determine the best land use for it.

Percentage chance of abandonment due to lack of services varies by zone type:

- Ind: 30%
- Com: 35%
- Res: 15%

Industrial Development Specifics

The development of Industrial zones is somewhat different from *SimCity 2000* and *SimCity Classic*. One difference is the addition of agricultural development, which is very low density. You can get a lot of Industrial development with little infrastructure if much of it is agricultural, but the main advantage of agricultural land is that it looks nice. All those barns and fields. Peaceful and unpolluting. Not like the bustling city that will replace it if you have your way, eh, Mayor? Such is the price of progress.

Nonagricultural industry is classified as either "dirty" or "clean" with the obvious advantages going to clean industry. One of the main challenges of *SimCity 3000* is to build a city that eventually becomes more and more clean industrially, thereby reducing pollution and raising land values.

Types of Industry

Agriculture develops in low-density industrial zones away from many roads and heavy pollution. It appears as barns, crops, and pastures. Agricultural land doesn't produce much Residential demand and will upgrade if conditions surrounding it change. Agriculture has about a 90 percent chance of developing if large areas of land are zoned low-density Industrial, there are low air and water pollution and low land values, and fewer than three edges of the zone have roads. (If you pass the Farmer's Market ordinance, the percentage chance of agriculture developing, if all other conditions are met, is 100 percent)

Because the size of a farm ranges from 8 × 8 to 8 × 18 tiles, a road through potential farmland can stop agriculture from developing. There must be at least an 8 × 8 block of low-density Industrial land having at least one edge not in contact with a road. If these conditions are met, a farm may develop.

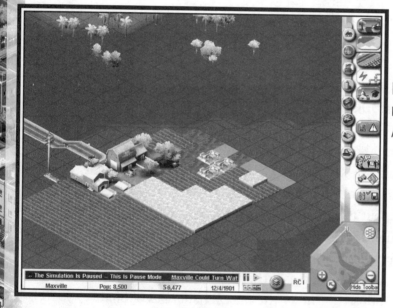

FIG. 6-16. FARM LAND MAY DEVELOP IF ALL THE CONDITIONS ARE RIGHT.

Dirty industry produces high pollution and low technology, which is displayed in your city literally as dirty-looking buildings with spewing smokestacks and noise. Dirty industry is the most prevalent industry available at the beginning of the twentieth century and will continue to develop if EQ levels are too low to sustain clean industry development. Examples of "dirty" industry include mines, factories, propane farms, furnaces, sludge fields, and so on.

Fig. 6-17. This industry is spewing out all kinds of pollution, but at least it's keeping the economy going.

Clean industry produces low amounts of pollution and high technology. It's displayed as office parks and clean-looking, high-tech buildings. Clean industry becomes more common after the middle of the twentieth century—starting about 1950 or so, and is more likely to develop in cities with high EQ and high land values. Other factors to consider include the passing of certain ordinances intended to promote clean industry or discourage dirty industry. The maximum percentage of Industry that can be clean in a city is 100 percent. Examples of clean industry include software development firms, industrial labs, research companies, warehouses, and so on.

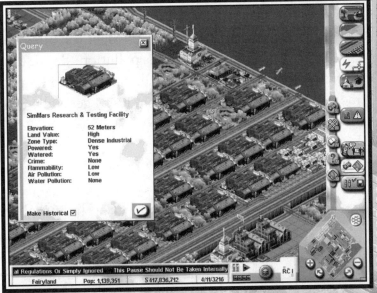

Fig. 6-19. As time goes on, with higher land values and higher EQ, cleaner industry will grow, meaning less pollution, greater health for your Sims, higher land values, and more tax revenue.

There are circumstances in which it becomes impossible to build any industry; for instance, if ordinances have been passed preventing dirty industry from building, but the EQ of your city is too low to sustain any more clean industry.

How Clean Industry Ratios Are Determined

Several factors influence the ratio of clean to dirty industry:

- The simulation year
- Global EQ
- Pollution
- Ordinances

In any given year, a certain ratio of clean to dirty industry is possible. At the beginning of the twentieth century, this ratio largely favors dirty industry. Over time, the percentage of clean industry that can develop increases. Whether the maximum clean to dirty ratio is attained depends on the global EQ of the city, which, in turn, is determined largely by the placement of schools, universities, libraries, etc. Certain ordinances also help maintain the global EQ of your Sims.

One pretty good strategy is to start educational development early, since Sims tend to inherit their initial EQ at birth from their parents—actually from the average EQ of the city. Starting early with schools and other measures designed to increase EQ assures that your city will convert to clean industry to the maximum allowed per year. For more information on how EQ works, see the section in Chapter 12: Demographics entitled "Meet the Sims, Meet Their Needs."

Another determining factor is pollution. Because it lowers land values and LE (Life Expectancy), which may indirectly affect EQ, pollution can prevent clean industry from developing. Clean industry generally looks for higher land values as well as higher EQ.

Ordinances

Several ordinances have a direct effect on Industrial demand. These are listed in Table 6-7. Most ordinances encourage clean industry. Ultimately, your city will be more successful if it can encourage the development of clean industry, thereby eliminating pollution, which can drive down land values and drive people away.

Some ordinances encourage a clean industry directly, such as the Tourism Promotion Ordinance. Others encourage industry by offering tax incentives or discourage dirty industry by legislation aimed at reducing pollution. Ordinances such as the Electronics Job Fair and Public Access encourage clean industry by increasing EQ, a prime factor in the development of clean industry.

TABLE 6-7: ORDINANCES THAT DIRECTLY AFFECT CLEAN VS. DIRTY INDUSTRIAL DEVELOPMENT

Ordinance	When Available	Cost
Conservation Corps	1915	§.0003/Sim
Industrial Pollution Impact Fee	1900 + Developed Industrial titles > 500	$0.000023/Sim
Clean Industry Association	1930	§.00039/Sim
Clean Air	1950	§0.0002/Sim
Electronics Tax Incentive	1950	§0.0003/Sim
Aerospace Tax Incentive	1960 + Airport	§0.0003/Sim
Electronics Job Fair	1970	§0.0003/Sim
Biotech Tax Incentive	1980	§.0003/Sim
Sponsor Public Access Cable	1980	§0.0003/Sim

Ordinances to discourage dirty industry, such as the Clean Air Ordinance, can have the effect of reducing Industrial demand overall if they push the ratio of clean to dirty industry beyond the maximum amount currently available. The maximum ratio of clean industry to dirty is determined by the EQ and the current year. Clean industry becomes more prevalent over time with rising levels of education.

Ordinance Costs

Most of the ordinances in Table 6-7 drain some money from your coffers; one actually generates income (Industrial Pollutant Impact Fee). The amount depends on the ordinance. For a more complete explanation of these and other ordinances, see Chapter 15.

Chapter 7
Power

Without power, a city is dead. Zones won't grow. Existing buildings will quickly be abandoned. Power, in the form of electricity, is the most important resource you can provide to your city, because without it nothing will grow. Oh, sure, you can plant lots of trees. But this isn't *SimForest*.

One of the first major tasks when you begin a new city is to provide it with at least one power plant by choosing from the Build Utilities menu and the Power Plants button. Depending on the time period and other conditions, you may be able to select from among any of eight power source buildings, or even work out a deal with a neighbor to purchase power.

Knowledge is another kind of power, so it might help to know as much as possible about how power works in *SimCity 3000*. In this chapter, we'll discuss:

- Sources of power
- Power distribution
- Power consumption
- Ordinances that affect power consumption
- Buying and selling power

Sources of Power

Choosing power sources for your city is generally a matter of weighing costs and benefits. Each plant has advantages and disadvantages. The factors that you want to consider are:

- Monthly capacity (output)
- Cost
- Pollution
- Land value (NIMBY/YIMBY) effects

Pollution affects a specific radius around the power plant. The effect gradually diminishes to zero at the outer edge of the radius. But, these effects can be cumulative within a specific area. This means that if you cluster your Coal power plant around a lot of dirty industry, the local effect on land values will be multiplied due to the proximity of so many polluting structures clustered together. The total pollution, city wide, will remain the same, but locally, land values will plummet. For this reason, many mayors may opt to keep buildings with strong negative local pollution and NIMBY effects isolated from other zones, also choosing to build smaller, separated areas of industry if it is dirty industry.

TIP

As it was in SimCity 2000, so it is today. You can avoid a lot of the negative effects of pollution from your power plants and dirty industry by placing them near the edge of the map, so that up to half their pollution will simply go harmlessly into someone else's backyard.

FIG. 7-1. PUTTING YOUR WORST POLLUTERS AT THE EDGE OF THE MAP IS A WAY OF AVOIDING NEGATIVE EFFECTS.

Table 7-1 shows this information for each of the power plants available in *SimCity 3000* as well as for power lines.

Power Plants

TABLE 7-1. POWER PLANT CAPACITY

Power Plant	Cost	MW-H/Month	Cost/MW	Year Available	Effects
Coal	5,000	6,000	.83	1900	pollution, NIMBY
Oil	8,500	7,000	1.21	1900	pollution, NIMBY
Gas	4,500	3,000	1.5	1955	NIMBY
Nuclear	20,000	16,000	1.25	1960	NIMBY, danger of meltdown
Wind	250	200	1.25	1980	output varies, better on top of hill, minor NIMBY
Solar	15,000	5,000	3	1985	NIMBY
Microwave	30,000	14,000	2.14	2020	NIMBY
Fusion	50,000	50,000	.6	2050	NIMBY
Waste-to-Energy	25,000	70	357.14	2000	pollution, NIMBY, garbage reduction
Power Line	15 per tile	—	—	1900	—
Neighbor Connect	2,000	variable	variable	1900	—

*MW-h = megawatt-hour

Following are the NIMBY effects on land values of the various power subsystems:

TABLE 7-2. NIMBY EFFECTS OF POWER PLANTS

Subsystem	Residential	Commercial	Industry	All Other
Power Line	-15	-15	N/A	N/A
Coal Power Plant	-90	-70	-15	-15
Oil Power Plant	-70	-55	-15	-15
Gas Power Plant	-60	-40	-9	-14
Microwave Power Plant	-50	-18	-7	-12
Nuclear Power Plant	-110	-80	-30	-12
Fusion Power Plant	-50	-18	-7	-12
Solar Power Plant	-35	-14	-4	-9
Wind Generator	-15	-14	-4	-9
Waste-to-Energy Plant	-35	-15	-8	-12

Pollution effects (Air, Water, Garbage)

As described above, pollution for each building is measured by a maximum effect, which is present on tiles immediately surrounding the building in question and which gradually dissipates over a specified radius. However, because these effects are cumulative based on the proximity of other polluting buildings, the actual effect on land value on any given tile may be far greater than would appear from simply reading the numbers. Even a relatively low-polluting building, if clustered with many other such buildings, can have a significant effect on surrounding land. What is true of air pollution is also true of water pollution, which also has a maximum value that dissipates over a set radius of effect. However, garbage is simply a certain amount produced per month and should be handled by appropriate means such as landfills and incinerators, or a Neighbor Deal.

TABLE 7-3. POLLUTION OUTPUT OF POWER PLANTS

Subsystem	Air	Water	Garbage
Power Line	0	0	0
Coal Power Plant	5,000	3,000	50
Oil Power Plant	3,000	1,750	50
Gas Power Plant	2,000	1,250	50
Microwave Power Plant	50	100	50
Nuclear Power Plant	25	50	50
Fusion Power Plant	25	25	50
Solar Power Plant	0	0	0
Wind Generator	0	0	0
Waste-to-Energy Plant	2,500	1,500	0

Power Plant Capacity

Every power source puts out a fixed amount of power per month, with the exception of Wind Generators, which vary depending on conditions and placement. Every building consumes power, including special buildings such as Seaports and Airports. The total power required for any city is the aggregate of all building and zone power consumption and is measured monthly.

The output of a power source is measured in megawatts (MW-h) per month, so, as Table 7-1 reveals, a Coal plant produces 6,000 MW-h per month while a Gas plant only delivers 3,000 MW-h per month. Each power plant provides all the power it can. If more than one power plant is connected to the power grid, each will deliver a proportion of the total power needed. For instance, if there is only one power plant with a capacity of 6,000 MW-h and the city is drawing 3,000 MW-h per month, that power plant will be operating at 50 percent capacity. Adding another power plant of equal capacity would cause the new plant to take over some of the first one's load. Therefore, both plants would operate at 25 percent capacity.

Power Plant Overload Conditions

If a city requires more power than the power plants can deliver, those plants may begin to operate at above 100 percent capacity (to a maximum of 110 percent), attempting to provide as much power as possible. However, once a power plant begins operating at more than 100 percent capacity, it runs the risk of exploding. You'll receive repeated messages regarding the dangerous condition of your power plant. You can safely run a power plant over capacity for a year and a half, but after that the probability that it will explode increases until, by two and a half years, it will definitely explode.

If a power plant explodes, it leaves rubble in its place. An exploding power plant will not normally damage nearby buildings. Any buildings depending on that plant's output will, however, suffer a loss of power. The one exception is in the case of Nuclear plants. When a Nuclear plant explodes, it adds radioactive pollution in a 20-tile radius. This will drive Sims out of that area until the radiation goes away *naturally*—which is basically *never*, though the developers of *SimCity* say "thousands of years."

Power Plant Life Spans

Power plants have a fixed life span. Also, they'll become less effective over time, so that during the latter half of their life span their capacity will gradually decrease. If they aren't replaced, power plants will turn to rubble when they grow. Table 7-4 shows the relative life span of each type of power plant and the time at which they begin to lose effectiveness. The point at which they begin to become less effective is called the "Decline Age" in the table. These figures are average figures, and each individual plant may vary slightly.

TABLE 7-4: POWER PLANT LIFE SPANS AND DECLINE AGES

Plant	Life Span	Decline Age
Coal	70	56
Oil	70	56
Gas	80	64
Microwave	80	64
Nuclear	60	48
Fusion	60	48
Solar	100	80
Wind	120	96
Waste-to-Energy	70	56

Power Plant Pros and Cons

Coal vs. Oil

FIG. 7-2. A COAL PLANT

In 1900, you only have two power plant choices—Coal and Oil. The Coal plant is very dirty and produces less power than the Oil plant does, but it costs considerably less. An examination of cost per MW-h shows that the Coal plant produces 6,000 MW-h for 5,000 Simoleons. That boils down to .83 Simoleons per MW-h capacity. The Oil plant produces 7,000 MW-h for 8,500 Simoleons—about 1.2 Simoleons per megawatt. So, you pay a third more for the Oil plant. If money is an issue, the Coal plant is probably preferable. However, if you take pollution into account, the Coal plant has a slightly lower air pollution effect but a higher water pollution effect. With the slightly higher output and lower air pollution, many players prefer to start with the Oil plant.

Gas

FIG. 7-3. GAS PLANT

Gas plants are very inefficient financially, costing 1.5 Simoleons per MW-h capacity. However, they're relatively clean and therefore don't cause air or water pollution. Because Gas plants produce very little power per plant, and because Nuclear plants are available only a few years later—with very large capacity and very efficient use of money—it may be preferable to wait for the Nuclear plants to appear. It takes over five Gas plants to equal the output of one Nuclear plant, and it would cost 4,500 Simoleons to build each as opposed to 20,000 to build the Nuclear plant. Gas plants do have a longer life span, however.

Nuclear

FIG. 7-4. NUCLEAR PLANT

Aside from the risk of meltdown—and the irradiating of a 20-tile radius of your city—Nuclear plants are perhaps the best power sources. They produce a very high output for a relatively low cost, and they don't pollute—so long as they don't blow up. However, efficiency isn't everything, and some mayors prefer to build lots of Solar plants until Microwave or fusion plants become available, thus eliminating potential Nuclear disaster.

Wind

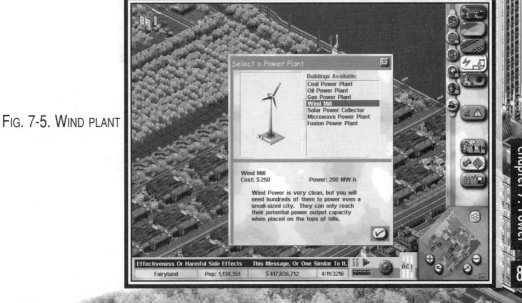

FIG. 7-5. WIND PLANT

Wind power is not particularly reliable, nor is it long lasting, but it is relatively cheap and nonpolluting. These windmills look cool, too, so there's not a great NIMBY effect. But, you have to place many windmills to provide much output. Some mayors will edit their terrain or use the Raise Land tool to create high, flat areas to use as "wind farms." At their most efficient, windmills generate 200 MW-h per month. Windmills are efficient financially, but inefficient in terms of land use. If you have vast tracts of high desert available around your city, a wind farm might make sense. But, building windmills in the lowlands, however appealing aesthetically, may not be the best investment.

Solar

FIG. 7-6. SOLAR PLANT

Solar power is clean and relatively efficient. However, it requires many Solar plants to equal the capacity of one good Nuclear facility. This means that Solar plants will quickly use up space. At some periods of a city's development, this may be acceptable. Other than the NIMBY effect, Solar plants have no real drawbacks; their long life spans are a definite plus. If space is a premium, however, Solar power is not the way to go, nor is it the best financial deal at 26 Simoleons per monthly megawatt capacity.

Microwave vs. Fusion

FIG. 7-7. MICROWAVE AND
FUSION PLANTS

Like the Nuclear plants, Microwave generators are pollution-free, though they do suffer from the NIMBY effect. They are costly compared with Nuclear plants. However, they do not bring with them the threat of nuclear meltdown and they last 20 years longer, on average. In the year 2050, fusion plants become available. These are equivalent in terms of game effects, but produce much more power at a slightly more efficient cost. Though fusion plants are the most expensive available, they also produce the most power in the smallest space. If your city has grown huge by the year 2050, fusion is the way to go.

Power Distribution

Power flows from a power plant through power lines, zones, and buildings. Any zone within two tiles of a power source or other powered zone or building will also receive energy, even if it doesn't yet have any buildings on it. This means that you can build an entire city without ever laying a power line. If two powered zones are within four tiles of each other, electricity will conduct between them. To cross water, however, a cable must be laid across a bridge if the distance is four tiles or more.

Although it's *possible* to build a city without any power lines, this may not be the best choice, particularly early in the game when you're trying to attract Sims to live in your city. A commonly used, effective strategy is to build the polluting power plant at the edge of the map, away from your newly zoned city, and use power lines to bring the power to where it's needed.

Power doesn't conduct through nonbuilding objects such as trees, Sims, vehicles, roads, rubble, or ashes, though the four-tile rule still applies. For instance, power will flow between two zones separated by a road, but if the road is more than four tiles wide, power won't conduct across it.

A tile is either powered or unpowered. If an unpowered tile contains a zone, building, or power line, it will be considered in a blackout condition—this includes abandoned buildings, empty zone tiles, and buildings under construction (none of which actually consume power). A graphic indication of the blackout condition will appear over the affected tile or building. In blackout conditions:

- Undeveloped zoned tiles won't develop.
- Developed zoned tiles will become abandoned.
- Unpowered puzzle zones (Airport, Seaport, landfill, etc.) won't develop.
- Unpowered water supply sources won't provide water.

Laying Power Lines

FIG. 7-8. ALTHOUGH YOU MIGHT NOT NEED TO LAY POWER LINES OFTEN, THEY DO COME IN HANDY SOMETIMES.

> **NOTE**
>
> SC2000 NOTE: POWER LINES OPERATE QUITE DIFFERENTLY IN SIMCITY 3000 THAN THEY DID IN PREVIOUS VERSIONS. FOR INSTANCE, POWER LINES BUILT INSIDE ANY ZONED AREAS WON'T BE REPLACED BY BUILDINGS. HOWEVER, BECAUSE ANY ZONED AREA WITHIN TWO TILES OF A POWERED TILE IS CONSIDERED FULLY POWERED, IT SHOULD NEVER BE NECESSARY TO BUILD POWER LINES THROUGH A ZONE. IN SIMCITY 2000, IT WAS OFTEN HELPFUL TO BUILD POWER LINES INTO A ZONE TO PROMOTE FASTER DEVELOPMENT. THIS IS NO LONGER NECESSARY. IN FACT, YOU'LL WANT TO AVOID BUILDING POWER LINES ON ANY TILES WHERE YOU WANT DEVELOPMENT TO OCCUR.

It's important to know how power lines work. Each power line should start from a tile that has power—basically within two tiles of a power source or powered zone or building. Each power line begins and ends with a terminus. Power lines have right of way and must be bulldozed if you wish to build anything on the tile they occupy. Remember, in order to be offered a power deal with a neighbor, you'll need to run a power line to that neighbor. Power lines can cross roads, as long as the road passes between the power line towers.

Power Consumption

Almost everything you create in your city consumes a certain amount of power—measured monthly. A building's query screen shows the amount of power consumed by a particular building. The drain on your power plants is cumulative. Clearly, the more buildings you place, the more power will be consumed. You can tell how your power plant is handling the load by querying the plant and reading what percentage of its capacity it is using.

Ordinances

There are really only two ordinances you can use to affect the power usage and efficiency of your city. These are Stairway Lighting (available 1930) and Power Conservation (available 1970). These ordinances effectively decrease power consumption in your city at a cost to your city's coffers. (In reality, they add to the power plant capacity, but this is done behind the scenes, in the simulation layer of the program.)

Stairway Lighting costs §0.0001/building, whereas Power Conservation costs §0.0001/Sim plus five Simoleons for each power plant in operation.

For more information about these ordinances, see Chapter 15: Ordinances.

Buying and Selling Power

Your neighbors can be either providers of power or customers for your excess power. Once you establish a power connection to a neighbor (cost = §2,000), you may be offered a deal by one of the petitioners to either buy or sell power. Although you can build power connections to each of your neighbors, assuming you're connected to them by land, only one purchase and one sales deal can exist at any given time, and not with the same neighbor. You can build multiple power connections to the same neighbor for redundancy, in case of a disaster, perhaps. Redundant power connections have no additional value, however.

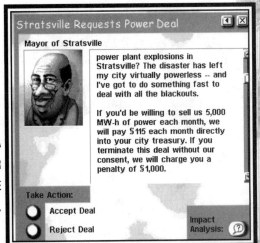

Stratsville Requests Power Deal

Mayor of Stratsville

power plant explosions in Stratsville? The disaster has left my city virtually powerless -- and I've got to do something fast to deal with all the blackouts.

If you'd be willing to sell us 5,000 MW-h of power each month, we will pay §115 each month directly into your city treasury. If you terminate this deal without our consent, we will charge you a penalty of §1,000.

Take Action:

○ Accept Deal

○ Reject Deal

Impact Analysis:

FIG. 7-9. MAKING A POWER DEAL WITH YOUR NEIGHBOR MAY TURN OUT TO BE MUTUALLY BENEFICIAL.

For more specifics of how the deals are structured, see Chapter 16: Neighbor Deals.

Pros and Cons of Buying and Selling Power

To decide whether a particular neighbor deal is a good idea, assess its costs and benefits.

Selling Power Costs

- You risk increasing demands and the possibility of having to build more power plants, which cost you money and use up more space.
- You risk running out of power and paying a penalty if you default on the deal.
- You accept the NIMBY effect of the power plants in your city.
- You accept the pollution effects of the power plants in your city.

Selling Power Benefits

- You receive money.

Buying Power Costs

You pay money to receive power.

The money you pay monthly increases over time.

You pay a minimum fee even if you aren't actually using any power from the neighbor.

Buying Power Benefits

You have no NIMBY effect.

You have no pollution effect.

You save money and space by not having to build power plants.

Getting Information about Power

There are several tools available to allow you to find out more about power usage in your city. These include the Query tool, Power Map, Graph Window, the Power Chart, and various Utilities Advisor and Petitioner messages.

Query Tool

You can query ordinary buildings and power lines, power plants, and power connections to neighbors.

Buildings and Power Lines

This will let you find out whether power is running through the area.

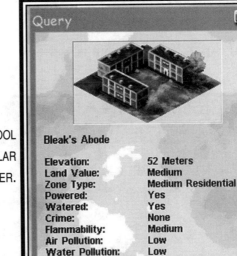

FIG. 7-10. USE THE QUERY TOOL TO FIND OUT IF A PARTICULAR STRUCTURE IS RECEIVING POWER.

Power Plants

Capacity: MW-h (megawatts per hour)
Usage: Low (0–40 percent), Medium (41–65 percent), High (66–100 percent), Dangerously High (101–110 percent)

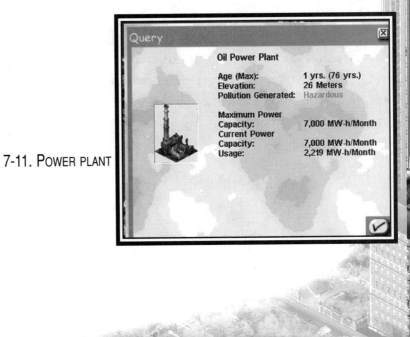

7-11. POWER PLANT

Power Connection to Neighbor

You can find out where a power line leads and whether it is powered.

FIG. 7-12. NEIGHBOR CONNECTION

Power Map

The Power Map is available from the View Data menu and shows which areas of your city that are powered or unpowered. Areas that are connected to the power grid, including unpowered zones and buildings that are in the grid, will show in one color while all other areas show in another color (colors will vary depending on your system.)

FIG. 7-13. POWER MAP

Power in the Graph Window

Access the city graph from the Data View. Check the Power Percentage checkbox to view your city's power usage over time in the line graph.

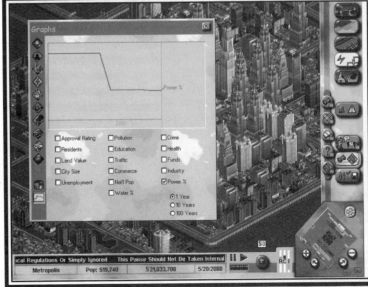

FIG. 7-14. POWER IN THE GRAPH
WINDOW

Power Chart

Use Data View and click the radio button next to Electricity to view either a bar or pie chart of your city's power sources. It lists each type of power source and the percentage of the city's power it provides.

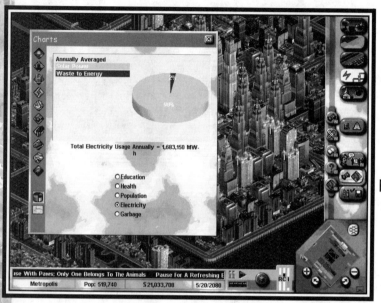

FIG. 7-15. POWER CHART

Chapter 8
Transportation

Sims have many needs. They need power, water, houses, jobs ... and they need transportation. Sims must get from here to there, to shop and commute, and to return home. In fact, transportation is so critical to the Sims' daily lives that they won't build anything unless it's within a few tiles of a road, railroad tracks, an airport, or any other means of movement.

There are three basic kinds of transportation in *SimCity 3000*:

- Public Transportation: roads and highways
- Mass Transportation: trains, buses, and subways
- Implied Transportation: Airports and, to some extent, Seaports and neighbor connections

In this chapter, we'll deal primarily with public and mass transportation. The types of transportation we have called "implied" have a significant effect on Commercial and Industrial demand levels, and they also allow more trips to be completed by out-of-town Sims. However, in this chapter, we'll focus most of our attention on roads and highways, rails, buses, and subways.

We've divided this subject into the following sections:

- Sims and How They Move
- Transportation Networks
- Funding
- Neighbor Connections
- Transportation-Related Ordinances

Sims and How They Move

Before looking at specific types of transportation you can build in your city, it's very valuable to understand why you would build one kind of network over another. To understand the "whys" of the situation, you need to understand Sim behavior. Two very specific factors affect the way Sims behave:

- Distance from transportation
- Trip generation and completion

Distance from Transportation

Sims have their preferences, and they can be pretty adamant at times. Sims won't build anything unless it's within a certain distance of some form of transportation. You must keep this in mind when zoning and building roads and other means of transportation.

The distance from transportation that a Sim will build depends on the type of zone:

Residential: four tiles
Commercial: three tiles
Industrial: five tiles

Agriculture: any part of the development must be within five tiles. (However, fields can be up to 8 × 18 in size for any individual farm, and multiple farms can stretch indefinitely if the proper conditions exist.)

This means at least one edge of a building must be within these limits. If a building is three tiles by three tiles, only the closest edge needs to be within the allowable distance. The other part of the building can be farther away and the Sims will still come and go as they please.

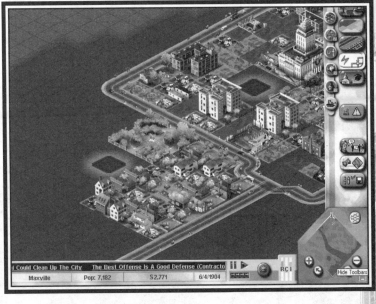

FIG. 8-1. IN THIS RESIDENTIAL ZONE, SIMS ARE WILLING TO TRAVEL FIVE TILES TO THE HIGHWAY.

NOTE

SC2000 NOTE: IN SIMCITY 2000, EACH ZONE REQUIRED THE SAME THREE-TILE DISTANCES TO TRANSPORTATION, WHICH MADE DESIGNING CITIES OFTEN A MATTER OF CREATING GRIDS THAT WERE SIX TILES WIDE, WITH TRANSPORTATION ON EITHER SIDE. THIS STRATEGY WON'T BE THE MOST EFFICIENT IN SIMCITY 3000.

TIP

THE SHUTTLE ORDINANCE CAUSES ALL TRANSPORTATION DISTANCES TO INCREASE BY ONE, MEANING THAT RESIDENTIAL BECOMES FIVE, COMMERCIAL BECOMES FOUR, AND INDUSTRIAL BECOMES SIX. THE SHUTTLE ORDINANCE IS ALWAYS AVAILABLE IF YOU HAVE MASS TRANSIT. HOWEVER, FOR THE SHUTTLE ORDINANCE TO TAKE EFFECT, YOU MUST HAVE TRAIN, BUS, OR SUBWAY SERVICE IN YOUR CITY.

When building your city's transportation network, you should keep these values in mind. Remember, every road, rail, or other transport tile you place on your map is going to cost you in monthly maintenance. Therefore, creating an *efficient* transportation system will pay off in the end. Don't overbuild. Plan ahead, but only place the transportation you need. As you expand your zones, you can expand roads and other transportation infrastructure.

Building Efficient Transportation Grids

Along with distancing your Residential and Commercial zones from pollution, the most important factor when designing your city is figuring out the distance Sims will travel to reach transportation. Does this mean that you should get out your slide rule and calculate the mathematically perfect, symmetrical layout that will pack the most people into your city? Sure, if that's what you want. But there are some other ways to approach city design.

One way is to build grids that are somewhat larger than you might think necessary. For instance, suppose, after enacting the Shuttle Ordinance, your Residential Sims will go five tiles to reach transportation. So, logically, a road surrounding a 10 × 10-tile area would seem to be a pretty good grid to build. Or, perhaps simply two parallel roads separated by 10 tiles, and with a cross street every 20 tiles.

FIG. 8-2. SOMETIMES YOU CAN GRID LARGER AREAS AND FILL IN WITH PARKS, WATER, AND POLICE.

There are good reasons for building a slightly larger grid. First, buildings only need to have one edge within the allowable transportation distance. This means that a larger building can be built with most of its area beyond that distance. Moreover, if buildings don't develop, the grid leaves room for water, parks, and police stations, thereby increasing land value in diverse ways.

For one thing, parks and police stations have YIMBY effects. Parks reduce effective pollution by adding a zero to the averaging of local pollution, which actually has a significant effect. Water will do the same while also producing a positive terrain effect that stretches over several tiles. Police stations lower crime, and if the crime falls below a certain threshold, which it should, then you get a land value boost from that. Also, Police stations don't have to be near transportation, so they can be built in the middle of a zone.

What's the bottom line? There's more than one way to grid a city and sometimes the obvious method isn't necessarily the best way.

Trip Generation and Completion

Another fundamental element of *SimCity* is the concept of trip generation. What this means is that Sims in any particular zone will, for reasons known only to the Sims themselves, decide to set out on a trip to another zone. The rationale is that Sims at home will set out to go to work or shop, or even to visit friends … that sort of thing. And Sims in other zones will set out on trips home, or elsewhere. When a Sim begins a trip, he or she will go only so many "steps" before giving up. Each traveling Sim has a specific destination zone in mind when he or she begins. The destination zone is determined by percentages:

TABLE 8-1. MAXIMUM ALLOWABLE TRIP DISTANCES

From	To Residential	To Commercial	To Industrial
Residential	10	40	100
Commercial	70	80	100
Industrial	50	70	100
Mixed or All	33	66	100

From a statistical point of view, trips are generated once per month from a percentage of existing Residential, Commercial, or Industrial buildings in the city. The trip begins when a Sim looks for transportation from its starting point. As detailed above, that distance will depend on what zone the trip begins from. Assuming the Sim finds suitable transportation within the allowable distance, the

NOTE

THE NUMBERS IN TABLE 8-1 REPRESENT THE STARTING PERCENTAGES OF TRIP GENERATION. HOWEVER, AS TIME PASSES, COMMERCIAL DEMAND WILL GRADUALLY INCREASE WHILE INDUSTRIAL DEMAND DECREASES. TRIP GENERATION PERCENTAGES WILL ALSO CHANGE IN ACCORDANCE WITH THIS SHIFT FROM COMMERCIAL TO INDUSTRIAL.

trip begins. If suitable transportation is not found, the trip is considered a failure. If trips continue to fail from a particular building, it will soon become abandoned.

When trips are calculated, the simulation starts with a base cost (variable; for example, eight), then finds the maximum distance that the Sim can travel. This distance is set based on the destination (see Table 8-1). As trips proceed, the maximum cost (base cost times maximum distance) is whittled away by travel. As the traveling Sim crosses a tile, the travel cost is calculated using the tile's base cost, modified by current conditions such as traffic congestion; that number is added to the real cost. Congestion can add up to the base cost again (so if a highway tile trip value is 1, it can cost 8 with no traffic and 16 with maximum traffic. A road tile would cost 3 times 8 plus 8). See Table 8-2 for the per-tile cost of each type of transportation.

When the Sim gets to an intersection, there's a "sheep factor" that causes the traveling Sim to attempt to go the most congested way. Why doesn't this end up with all thwarted trips? Travel uses an "exhaustive algorithm." If the Sims can't get where they want to go one way, they will backtrack and try another way, and keep trying until they either reach their goal or determine that there's no way to get there and give up. But the consequence is that some trips will fail when the added cost per tile uses up their maximum allocation for that trip (as seen in Table 8-2).

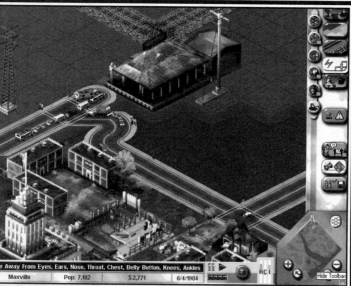

FIG. 8-3. SIMS IN TRAFFIC FOLLOW THE HERDING INSTINCT.

Taking Steps

For a trip to be successful, not only do Sims have to find acceptable transportation, but the trips must be completed within a certain number of "steps." Table 8-1 shows the maximum number of allowable steps from and to each zone type. Table 8-2 shows the number of steps used for each transit method, and Table 8-3 shows the maximum distances a Sim could travel under ideal conditions using each of these transit methods.

TABLE 8-2. COST IN STEPS FOR TRANSIT METHODS

Transit Type	Cost in Steps
Road Tile	4
Road Tile (once on a bus)	3
Highway Tile	2
Rail, Bus, and Subway Station (on/off)	6
Rail, Subway, Rail ≥ Subway Tiles	.6
Off/On-ramp	3
Potholed Roads	32
Traffic Effect	Variable

TABLE 8-3. RELATIVE MAXIMUM DISTANCES (TILES TRAVELED) PER TRANSIT TYPE

Transit Type	R–R	R–C	R–I	C–R	C–C	C–I	I–R	I–C	I–I
Road	3	13	33	23	26	33	16	23	33
Highway*	4	34	94	64	74	94	44	64	94
Bus^	1	16	46	31	36	46	21	31	46
Rail/Subway^	3	53	153	103	120	153	70	103	153

* Includes one on-ramp and one off-ramp (-6)

^ Includes two station transfers (-8)

As you can see from Table 8-2, every type of transportation tile uses up a Sim's available steps toward its destination. Driving on an ordinary road costs four steps per tile, while the highway only costs two steps per tile. Getting on and off the highway costs three steps (three each time the Sim uses the on/off-ramp). Mass transit costs six steps per station (rail, bus, or subway), but is the most efficient method of movement otherwise (costing only .6 per additional square). If a Sim is just driving around the block, it's more efficient to take the car (or maybe walk). However, using mass transit, particularly rail and subway, has the effect of lengthening the distance that Sims can go and still carry out successful trips.

Note that Sims will only use one form of mass transit for a particular trip. They won't take the bus to the subway station, then get on the subway to go somewhere else. Nor will they take a train or subway, then take a bus from there. They will drive a car to the subway or train station, or even to a bus stop.

FIG. 8-4. IF YOUR SIMS ARE WILLING TO USE MASS TRANSPORTATION, THEY CAN TAKE LONGER TRIPS TO AND FROM WORK.

You can see from Table 8-1 that Sims will travel farthest to reach Industrial zones. This is helpful because you want to keep Industrial zones away from Residential zones. Examining Table 8-2, which lists the actual step costs for each type of transit, allows you to draw some conclusions about how far Sims are willing to travel.

For instance, a trip from a Residential zone to an Industrial one must be completed within approximately 33 road tiles, under ideal conditions. Sims won't complete the trip if they must go any farther. However, if there is traffic congestion, this number may dwindle considerably.

Yet if mass transit is used exclusively, a Sim could conceivably travel 153 tiles (four for each station and .6 for each tile crossed). If the trip is a combination, the results will be in between. For instance, suppose the Sim has to drive 10 tiles to the train station and then travels another 10 tiles from the destination station to work. That's 60 road steps under ideal conditions. Then, the train trip costs four steps per station and .6 per tile on the train. So the maximum distance that can be traveled in this case is 73 steps (20 on the road and 53 on the train, plus two station stops of 4 steps each).

The Importance of Tripping

Whenever a trip is unsuccessful, that lack of success is noted as feedback about the building from which that trip originated. Stated another way, each building is only effective if the Sims who use it (to live in, shop in, or work in) can get from it to other places in the city. If too may trips are unsuccessful, it is an indication that the Sims can't get on with their daily lives effectively, and will tend to drive that building toward the abandoned state. On the other hand, feedback from successful trips tells the simulation that this building is a happening place and that the Sims are leading active, productive lives.

Other Variables that Affect Trips

Two other factors that affect trips:

- Traffic congestion
- Degradation of transportation

Traffic Congestion

The internal trip generator in *SimCity 3000* tracks successful trips and tends to repeat the use of successful paths. This results in the establishment of "preferred" routes, much the way it happens in real cities. And, also as in real cities, this results in traffic congestion. As more and more traffic attempts to cross the same transit tiles, you end up with traffic jams, which actually increase the number of steps it takes to move across the same tiles. Stated another way, a road that normally costs three steps per tile can cost much more per tile when congested. This effect is cumulative, because a stretch of congested road makes for a much longer trip. Sims, like folks everywhere, hate to get stuck in traffic. Sims have an "annoyance factor" that builds up until the situation becomes intolerable to them. If the annoyance factor is high enough, a Sim will look for an alternate route rather than following the herd. If they're stuck too long, they may turn around and go home, causing the trip to fail.

Using mass transit (rail, buses, or subways) can have a significant effect on traffic density and is highly encouraged. When Sims use rail or subway transportation, then they're not on the roads and highways.

Degradation of Transportation

Funding for the Transportation Department also can have an effect on trip success or failure because roads will tend to degrade over time if funding is not kept high enough. Roads dotted with potholes will slow traffic down by adding to the per-tile trip count for affected roadways. The simulation is even more devious in that it tends to cause heavily used road tiles to become damaged first, if funding is insufficient. This, of course, has a greater impact on your city and its Sims than a simply random effect would have. The solution to this problem is simple enough: Fund the Transportation department adequately, and you won't have any problems.

More Facts

Here are a few more subtle elements of trip generation and completion that you may like to know:

- Trips from Industrial zones will always use rail, if available.
- Trips originating in Residential and Commercial zones may choose to use mass transit.
- Passing the Subsidize Mass Transit Ordinance significantly increases the likelihood that Residential and Commercial traffic will use mass transit, thereby leading to a much higher percentage of completed trips and a much more effective city transportation network.
- Neighbor connections via road, rail, or subway also add to completed trips, so it's a good idea to have connections to neighbors. This is especially true early in the life of a city if you've isolated your Industrial zones from the others and may have reason to worry that all necessary trips aren't going to be completed. With a single neighbor connection, you can add to the chances of successful trips from an Industrial zone placed near the edge of the map.

● Another way to ensure successful trips is to place some very small Industrial zones within your Residential areas. If they are small enough, the pollution effect shouldn't drive down land values too much and the likelihood of successful trips increases.

FIG. 8-5. MAKE CONNECTIONS TO YOUR NEIGHBORS TO INCREASE THE NUMBER OF SUCCESSFUL TRIPS THAT ARE MADE.

Visual Feedback

You can get visual feedback on your city's transportation in several ways. The most reliable way is to look at the Traffic Density Map, but you also can zoom in to your city's streets and watch cars, trucks, and pedestrians move around. The more vehicles there are, the more dense the traffic. You also may notice that some vehicles are slower than others, and that vehicles will stop for pedestrians. All these effects slow down traffic, which potentially causes trips to fail. So, pay attention to what you observe.

You can get information about your mass transit system by using the Query tool on Bus, Train, and Subway Stations. You'll get statistics on the number of trips these methods of transit have generated each day, under "passengers".

FIG. 8-6. USE THE QUERY TOOL TO FIND OUT HOW YOUR MASS TRANSIT SYSTEM IS DOING.

Checking the Traffic Density Map

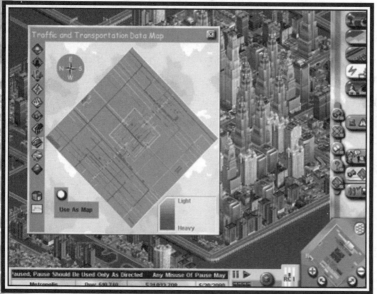

FIG. 8-7. THE TRAFFIC DENSITY MAP HELPS YOU SURVEY TRAFFIC FLOW AND IDENTIFY POTENTIAL GRIDLOCK.

Accessing the View Data section of *SimCity 3000* allows you to select the Traffic Density Map and see the areas of your city that have the most or least traffic.

Transportation Networks

Now that you know how and why Sims travel, let's look more closely at what transit networks are available.

There are also several types of buildings you can construct to support your network, some of which are offered automatically when the terrain (steep hills or water) warrants them:

- Bus Station
- Rail Station
- Subway Station
- Bridges
- Tunnels
- Subway » Rail Station

TABLE 8-5. TRANSIT ELEMENTS, AVAILABILITY, AND COST

Method	Year Available	Cost	Type
Road	Always	10	public
Highway	1940	150*	public
On/off-ramp	1940	75	public
Rail	Always	10	mass
Rail Station	Always	250	mass
Bus Station	1920	150	mass
Subway Tube	1910	150	mass
Subway Station	1910	500	mass
Rail » Subway	1910	500	mass

NOTE

*HIGHWAY COST IS PER TILE. A BLOCK OF HIGHWAY IS FOUR BLOCKS, OR $600. AFTER 1965, THE COST PER TILE DROPS TO $135, AND THE COST OF AN ONRAMP DROPS TO $68.

Roads

FIG. 8-8. ROADS ARE ESSENTIAL TO LIFE IN THE BIG (OR SMALL) SIMCITY.

Sims love their roads. All things being equal, they would love to hop in their cars and drive everywhere. Unfortunately, if you only build roads and nothing else, your city will soon become gridlocked and your Sims will become a grumpy lot indeed. Still, roads are essential building blocks, especially early. Theoretically, you could build a road-free city, but only after your city has become mature and has plenty of money to build subways and rails everywhere. You must build roads first, then tear them down in order to have a road-free city. This is impractical, so you may as well get used to placing a lot of roads around your city to begin with.

Each road tile you place costs you some money and adds to your monthly transportation maintenance costs. So, good city designers will consider efficient use of roads to service the most Sims.

Highways

Highways become available in 1940 and allow Sims to travel three times as fast as they do on roads. Highways are elevated thoroughfares, and can only be accessed by means of on- and off-ramps placed strategically along their length. Note that on/off-ramps work the same as they do in the real world, meaning that, for traffic to flow in both directions on the highway, you must build on/off-ramps on both sides to allow cars to enter and exit the highway going in both directions as shown in the image below.

FIG. 8-9. ON AND OFF-RAMPS FOLLOW LOGICAL RULES, JUST LIKE IN THE REAL WORLD.

Legal Travel

Travel must follow legal direction, using onramps as a real freeway would.

TIP

SIMS ALWAYS TRAVEL WITH A PARTICULAR DESTINATION ZONE IN MIND. BE SURE THAT AT LEAST ONE TRAIN STATION IS WITHIN APPROXIMATELY FOUR TILES OF EACH TYPE OF ZONE. FOR INSTANCE, IF A SIM SETS OUT ON A RAIL TRIP ORIGINATING FROM A RESIDENTIAL ZONE AND HEADED TO A COMMERCIAL ZONE, AND THERE ARE NO COMMERCIAL AREAS WITHIN APPROXIMATELY FOUR TILES OF A TRAIN STATION, THAT TRIP WILL FAIL. SO BE SURE THAT THERE IS AT LEAST ONE TRAIN STATION NEAR EACH TYPE OF ZONE.

Because Sims travel faster on highways, more trips can take place on them and those trips can extend a greater distance. There is a trip cost of three steps for each on or off-ramp, so for very short trips, roads are still more efficient. Highways are good for connecting distant areas of the same city, and highway connections to neighbors have a greater effect than ordinary road connections.

Rails

Rail transportation is very efficient, but Sims can't get on or off the train just anywhere they like, as they can with roads. They must board and exit trains at train stations, which should be placed strategically along the rail line. Since rail transportation is so efficient—five times as efficient as road transportation—it's a very good way to get Sims to travel long distances. For shorter distances, the four-step cost of each train station cuts into the efficiency of rail transportation.

FIG. 8-10. BE SURE YOUR TRAIN STATIONS ARE NEAR EACH OF THE RCI ZONES, OR SOME OF YOUR PASSENGERS WILL NEVER GET WHERE THEY ARE GOING.

Buses

Buses become available in 1920 and, like all mass transit options, help to reduce traffic congestion. However, buses have some advantages and disadvantages when compared with other mass transit. They aren't nearly as efficient, being only one-third more efficient than road travel and also requiring the usual four-step penalty per bus station. Bus stations also have a minor NIMBY effect. Their main advantage, however, is that they allow Sims to disembark at any point along their route.

Early in the game, buses are an efficient method of creating mass transit, since all you have to do is plop a couple of bus stations anywhere along a road route. Contrast this with having to build a rail or subway network, and you can see that it's the easiest form of mass transit and the most cost-effective early in the game.

FIG. 8-11. REMEMBER THAT SIMS CAN ONLY BOARD A BUS AT A BUS STOP, BUT THEY CAN GET OFF THE BUS ANYWHERE ON ITS ROUTE.

Subways

Subways are actually part of the overall rail system of your city, but they travel underground. Subways are more expensive to build and to maintain, but they allow you to create mass transit in densely packed cities without having to use up extra land to do so. Sims can only enter and exit subways via subway stations or rail-to-subway stations, with the usual four-step penalty per station. Although subways become available in 1910, they're probably a better option later in the game, when you have a larger city and there's money to build and maintain a large underground network.

You can add subway stations in either the above-ground or underground subway views. You can only add subway tubes when in the subway view. In the subway view, you'll see the underground portion of all subway stations as well as all subway tubes. Subway tubes will follow the contour of the ground above, so you won't be able to build tubes where the land is too steep.

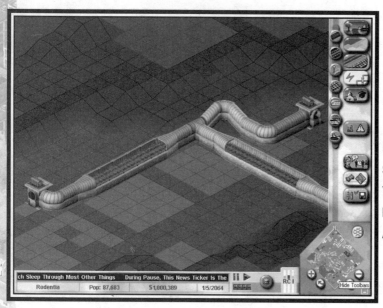

FIG. 8-12. BUILD YOUR SUBWAY NETWORK UNDER YOUR CITY FOR A GREAT METHOD OF MASS TRANSIT AND LAND SAVINGS, TOO.

It's somewhat harder to lay subways than roads, because when building roads over steep terrain, your engineers will automatically make necessary adjustments to make it work. With subways, these adjustments aren't possible, so the best strategy for designing the subway system is to stick to laying the tubes under roads and large, flat, built spaces.

Note that if you build a subway tube to the edge of the map, you'll be offered an opportunity to make a subway connection to a Neighbor. This connection has a similar effect to building a highway connection to a neighbor.

Bridges

Whenever you attempt to cross a body of water with a road, highway, or rail, you'll be offered the opportunity to build a bridge. You can decline if you like, but if you really want to get across that water, you may have to pay the price. Bridges are more expensive than ordinary transit tiles, so you may want to consider carefully whether you really need to cross that water, or if there's an alternate route. Bridges can only be built horizontally or vertically. You can't build a diagonal bridge. The kind of bridge depends on the type of transit you're building and the distance the bridge must travel.

FIG. 8-13. WHEN YOU TRY TO BUILD A ROAD, RAIL, OR HIGHWAY OVER WATER, YOU'LL HAVE A CHANCE TO BUILD A BRIDGE—BUT AT A COST.

Tunnels

Some land is too steep to allow you to build a road, highway, or rail. If you try to build into this kind of land, you'll be offered the opportunity to build a tunnel through it. Tunnels can help you get through mountainous terrain, but they do cost considerably more than ordinary transit tiles. In some cases, if no appropriate exit is possible, you'll be informed that the tunnel can't be built. As with bridges, it's a good idea to consider whether a tunnel is really necessary, or if there's an alternate way to get where you're going.

FIG. 8-14. WHEN YOU TRY TO BUILD A ROAD OR RAIL THROUGH A MOUNTAIN, YOU'LL BE GIVEN A CHANCE TO BUILD A TUN-NEL, IF CONDITIONS ARE RIGHT.

Table 8-6: Relative Bridge and Tunnel Costs

Transit	Normal	Bridge	Tunnel
Road	10	100	1000
Highway	600/block	1000	NA
Rail	10	100	1000

Funding Transportation

Every road, highway, rail, subway, bridge, and tunnel tile as well as every bus, train, or subway station you place in your city adds something to the monthly maintenance costs associated with your Transportation Department. These maintenance costs are divided into two departments: roads and mass transit. You must separately fund each of these departments. Table 8-7 shows the costs per tile of each of these transit elements. These costs will add up if you're wasteful, and the effects of underfunding can be unfortunate.

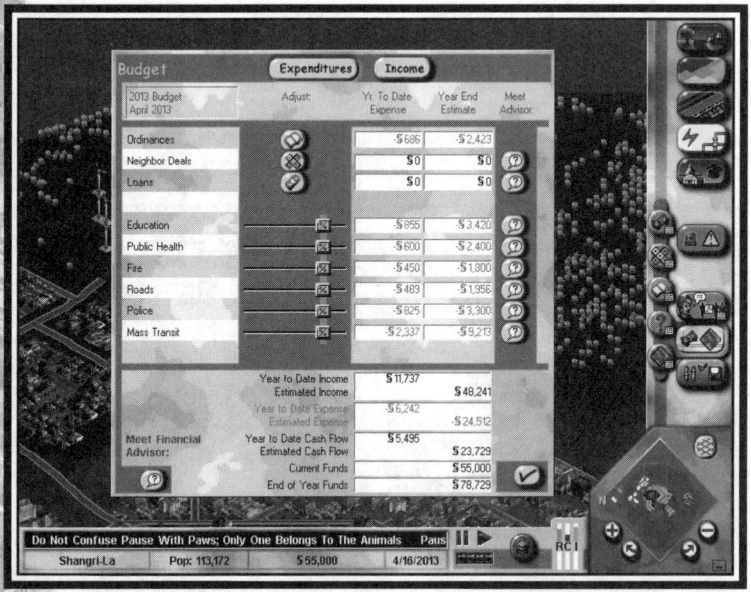

FIG. 8-15. WHATEVER TRANSPORTATION NETWORK YOU BUILD, DON'T FORGET TO PROVIDE IT WITH FUNDING.

TABLE 8-7. MONTHLY TRANSPORTATION MAINTENANCE COSTS

Transit	Cost/Month
Road	.02
Highway	.3
Rail	.01
Subway	.2
Bus Station	5
Rail Station	10
Subway Station	11
Rail ≥ Subway	11
Bridge	§1/50 tiles
Tunnel	§1/50 tiles

Funding Roads

The transportation slider, like all city budgets, can be set anywhere from zero to 120 percent. So, if you slide it all the way to the right, you're actually overfunding. However, you don't want to err on the other side and underfund your roads and highways. If you do so, you'll end up with roads and highways full of potholes, which will severely affect your Sims' travel plans. The lower your funding, the higher the percentage of roads and highways that will become damaged by potholes. To replace potholed tiles, you can either increase the budget, in which case the simulation will do it for you, or bulldoze the affected tiles and replace them.

Funding Mass Transit

If you fund mass transit between 100 percent and 110 percent of what is needed, there will be a very small added probability that Sims will take mass transit, if available, instead of driving their cars. Above 110 percent does nothing at all except trigger some news ticker messages that stroke your mayoral ego. However, the truth is, you're wasting money.

If you severely and chronically underfund your Transportation Department, you risk the possibility of a transit strike. The probability of a transit strike when the department is underfunded increases with the amount of underfunding and also increases over time. So the lower you set your funding for mass transit, and the longer you leave it there, the higher the probability of a strike occurring.

Mass Transit Strikes

If you should incur a mass transit strike:

- Picketers will protest in front of rail and subway stations.
- Petitioners representing the transit workers will appear on the Petitioner List demanding a 12 percent raise. The strike will last for two years, and, if you've done nothing, will end with the workers returning to their jobs.
- Your city will behave as if bus, rail, and subway transportation doesn't exist, which will affect traffic congestion. This in turn will affect Residential, Commercial, and Industrial demand because more trips will fail.

Ending a Strike

You have three options for ending a strike once it starts:

- Approve the 12 percent raise. Everyone will happily go back to work.
- Wait for two years until everyone gives up. Of course, if you continue to keep funding too low, the probability of another strike will continue to increase, starting at the base level for that funding level.
- Demolish every building associated with mass transit, which effectively fires everyone in that department. This includes all subway tubes and rails ... this approach is pretty severe, and one no sane mayor would entertain. Unless, of course, you just love to destroy things and throw money away, and there are easier ways to do that!

Obviously, this last option is pretty drastic and probably less desirable than just giving out the 12 percent raise or waiting the two years. Once mass transit is back in operation, however, it would behoove you to restore funding to full levels as soon as you can; otherwise you'll soon have another strike on your hands.

Neighbor Connections

FIG. 8-16. BUILD ROADS, RAILS, HIGHWAYS, OR SUBWAYS TO YOUR NEIGHBORS. YOU'LL BE GLAD YOU DID.

If you drag the road, highway, or rail icons off the edge of the city map, you'll be given the opportunity to create a connection with a neighboring city. Road connections with neighbors can increase Commercial demand by allowing more people to drive in from other cities. They'll also allow increased Simmigration to your city. Also, transportation connections to neighbors add to the trip count because Sims will travel to and from neighboring cities. Highway connections simply have a greater effect than road connections.

Rail connections also can increase Industrial demand because the rail system can transport goods between cities.

All three—road, highway and rail—connections allow you to create a garbage deal with a neighbor. Seaports also allow garbage deals to be struck.

Neighbor connections cost money, but they're generally worth it because of the added stimulation they give your economy.

TABLE 8-8. NEIGHBOR CONNECTION FEE

Connection	Fee
Road	§2,500
Highway	§5,000
Rail	§2,500
Subway	$4,000
Seaport	none
Water	§2,000
Power	§2,000

Transportation-Related Ordinances

There are several ordinances that can affect your transportation network. Table 8-9 gives a summary of these ordinances. For more detailed information, see Chapter 15: Ordinances.

TABLE 8-9. TRANSPORTATION ORDINANCES

Ordinance	Available	Monthly Cost	Pro	Con
Parking Fines	Always	+.00065 per Sim	Less traffic, Increases income	Decreases Aura
Shuttle Service	Always (but must have bus, rail, or subway service)	-§.008/Sim	+1 tiles to transport	Costs §
Crossing Guard	Always (but not petitioned until >250 road tiles exist)	-§.0005/Sim	Increases LE	Costs §; raises traffic 3%
Subsidize Mass Transit	1940 and bus, subway, or rail service exists	Mass transit revenues cut in half	Increases ridership	Reduces revenue
Alternate Day Driving	1950	-§.0001/Sim	Lowers traffic	Costs §; decreases Aura
Carpool Incentive	1980	-§.00065/Sim	Global traffic decreased 5%	Costs §

Chapter 9
Water, Water Everywhere...

Although water isn't as critical as electricity, it's a close second if you want a city that reaches its highest potential density. Without adequate water, zones won't grow past low density. Water also serves to lower the flammability of buildings, which in turn reduces the risk of devastating fires that can wipe out whole blocks at a time.

In this chapter we'll look at:

- Water structures and sources
- Water distribution
- Placing water on the map
- Ordinances
- Buying and selling water

Water Structures and Sources

FIG. 9-1. YOU'LL WANT TO PLACE WATER PUMPS AND WATER TOWERS EARLY TO ACHIEVE THE BEST RESULTS.

Table 9-1 shows a list of structures associated with water. For maximum efficiency, each of these structures needs to be connected to the water grid, and each (other than the water pipes) must be connected to the electrical grid. Remember, however, that each water structure will radiate water seven tiles out, so, in theory, you could simply build a lot of Water Towers and never actually put in any pipes.

TABLE 9-1. WATER STRUCTURES

Structure	Cost	Cubic Meters per Month	Available	Life Expectancy	Notes
Water Pipes	§5	NA	1900	NA	Water is spread seven tiles to either side of the water pipe
Pumping Station	§300	1,500	1900	110 years	Reduced to 20% effective if more than one tile from fresh water source; reduced efficiency if water is polluted; also reduced efficiency as it ages
Water Tower	§150	600	§1900	130 years	Reduced efficiency if water is polluted and as they age
Water Treatment Plant	§15,000	NA	1935	70 years	Reduces water pollution by up to 1.8m units each month citywide
Desalinization Plant	§1,500	5000	1965	100 years	Must be next to salt water; reduced efficiency if more than one tile from salt water, if water is polluted or as they age

Water can be obtained from several sources on any City Map. Rivers, streams, lakes, and sea coasts, as well as decorative water you can place on the map, are all sources of water. However, there's assumed to be an even layer of groundwater as well, so placing a Water Tower anywhere on the map will produce some water. All other water structures are far less efficient, or even useless, if they aren't placed near an appropriate water source.

There's also an additional NIMBY effect from the various water pumping subsystems. The following table shows the percentage hits on land value:

TABLE 9-2. NIMBY EFFECTS ON LAND VALUE

Subsystem	Residential	Commercial	Industrial	All Other
Water Pump	-5%	NA	NA	NA
Water Treatment Plant	-20%	-12%	-5%	-10%
Desalinization Plant	-20%	-12%	-5%	-10%
Water Tower	-10%	-2%	NA	NA

Pollution Density

Pollution (air, water, and garbage) for each building is measured by a maximum effect, which is present on tiles immediately surrounding the building in question and which gradually dissipates over a specified radius. However, because these effects are additive based on the proximity of other polluting buildings, the actual effect on land value on any given tile may be far greater than would appear from simply reading the numbers. Even a relatively low-polluting building, if clustered with many other such buildings, can have a significant effect on surrounding land. What is true of air pollution is true of water pollution, which also has a maximum value that dissipates over a set radius of effect. However, garbage is simply a certain amount produced per month, and should be handled by appropriate means, such as landfills and incinerators.

FIG. 9-2. LIKE AIR POLLUTION, WATER POLLUTION TENDS TO HAVE AN ACCUMULATING LOCAL EFFECT.

TABLE 9-3. POLLUTION OUTPUT FOR WATER STRUCTURES

Subsystem	Air	Water	Garbage
Water Pump	8	0	0
Water Treatment Plant	50	—	30
Desalinization Plant	50	0	30

Water is considered to be infinitely available, so you can't run out, no matter how many pumps you may place or how much your Sims consume. One limiting factor to water usage is water pollution. After 1935, it will be beneficial to place some Water Treatment Plants. For more information on water pollution, see Chapter 10: Pollution.

Life Span

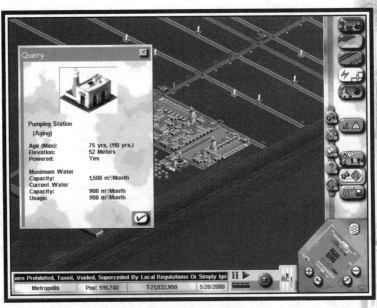

FIG. 9-3. WHEN YOU QUERY A
WATER STRUCTURE, YOU'LL SEE
ITS LIFE SPAN AND OTHER DATA.

Water structures have fixed life spans. They'll become less effective over time, so during the latter half of their life spans their capacity will gradually decrease. If they aren't replaced, water structures will eventually turn to rubble when they've grown too old. Table 9-4 shows the relative life span of each type of water structure and the time at which it begins to lose effectiveness. These figures are average figures, and each individual plant may vary slightly.

TABLE 9-4. WATER STRUCTURE LIFE SPANS AND DECLINE AGES

Plant	Life Span	Decline Age
Water Pump	110	55
Water Tower	130	65
Water Treatment Plant	70	64
Desalinization Plant	100	50

Water Distribution

To distribute water to your city, you must build some structure(s) for pumping water—Pumping Station, Water Tower, or Desalinization Plant (when they become available). These structures must be connected to the power grid, and they also must be connected by means of water pipes to the city water system.

Water distribution is similar to the distribution of power in the city in that all pumping sources distribute water over the grid to all buildings and zones, radiating from the source of the water. However, unlike electrical output, a pumping source's output may depend on the amount and kind of water available where it's placed. Also, zones don't conduct water as they do power. Only water structures and pipes conduct water.

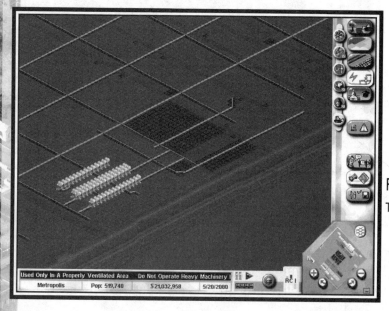

FIG. 9-4. THE WATER GRID DISTRIBUTES WATER TO YOUR CITY.

Water pumping facts:

- Water pumps must be powered to operate.
- Water Pumps must be connected to Water Pipes to distribute the water they produce.
- Pumping Stations can be placed anywhere, but if they're more than one tile from a fresh water source, their output is reduced by 80 percent. In some cases, you'll find that the terrain prevents placing a Water Pump within one tile of a suitable water source. In such cases, you might consider using the terrain lowering or terrain raising tools to create a suitable, level spot next to the water for your pump.
- Water Towers can be placed anywhere and are assumed to suck up water from deep underground aquifers—there's no advantage to placing a Water Tower near a water source.
- Water pumping structures have limited life spans and will begin to lose effectiveness at some point during that life span.

- Desalinization plants must be placed next to salt water or they're useless.
- Water pollution reduces the effectiveness of all Water Pumps.
- The only way to reclaim polluted water is to build Water Treatment Plants (available after 1935).
- Water pollution can be reduced by passing certain ordinances, by getting rid of polluting buildings, and by promoting more clean industry.

The Pipes View

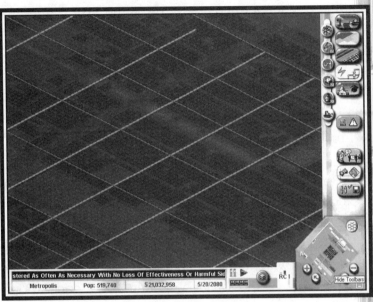

FIG. 9-5. IN THE PIPES VIEW, YOU CAN SEE YOUR WATER GRID AND THE PARTS OF YOUR CITY THAT ARE RECEIVING WATER.

Water won't be conducted from one building or zone to another without the use of Water Pipes (or nearby water structures), which you must place manually using the underground Pipes View. When you choose the Water Pipes tool, the view will automatically switch to the Pipes View. You'll see the following features in the Pipes View:

Water Pipes and pumping sources are all displayed.

Water sources will be blue.

Areas relevant to the water grid that are receiving water are blue.

Areas that are zoned or zoned and developed, but not receiving water, are orange.

All other tiles are gray or brown.

This view is a mirror image of the terrain above it. It shows terrain variations.

Pipes may be laid under roads, which will show up as gray tiles in the Pipes View.

If you have an area with a lot of steep terrain, it'll be much easier to lay the pipes under roads.

● Each Water Pipe will radiate water to any zone or building within seven tiles.

Water Consumption

Each building connected to the water grid will consume a certain amount of water. As water radiates from a pumping source through the grid, each building uses some water until there's none left. Any Water Pipes or buildings left over won't receive water. Trees, roads, tracks, subways, power lines, and other nonbuilding structures aren't considered to be part of the water grid. The water layer is updated by the simulation once each month.

If a building or zone doesn't receive water:

● Zones won't develop past low density, low- to medium-value buildings.
● Existing buildings of high value or medium- to high- density will become abandoned.
● The flammability rating of any building that isn't watered is higher by 25 percent. This isn't true of objects not on the grid, such as trees, roads, etc.

In addition to the Pipes View, several tools are available to help you find out more about water usage in your city. These tools include the Query tool, Water Supply Map, Graph Window, Water Chart, and various Utilities Advisor and Petitioner messages.

Query Tool

You can query ordinary buildings, zones, Water Pipes, water structures, and water connections to neighbors.

Buildings, Zones, and Water Mains

Click on a building or zone
to see whether it is watered.

FIG. 9-6. THE QUERY SCREEN
SHOWS WHETHER A BUILDING IS
RECEIVING WATER OR NOT.

Water Pumps

Maximum Capacity: 1,500 cubic meters/month
Current Capacity: Variable
Usage: Variable
Water Pollution Effect: Low/Medium/High/Unusable

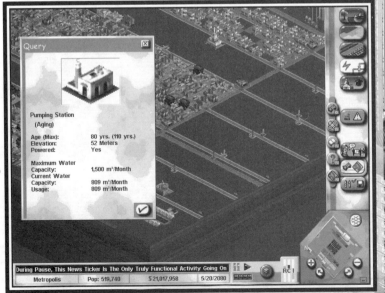

FIG. 9-7. WATER PUMP

Water Treatment Plant

Water Treated: Variable cubic meters/month
Connected to Water Mains: Yes/No

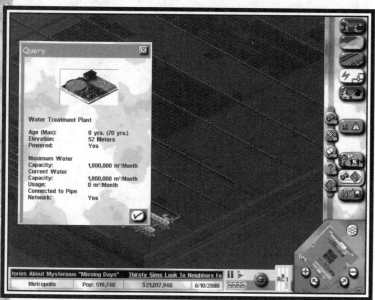

FIG. 9-8. WATER TREATMENT PLANT

Water Connection to Neighbor

Buying Water at Rate (in cubic meters/month)
Selling Water Rate
Trade Requirements (in cubic meters/month)

FIG. 9-9. NEIGHBOR
CONNECTION

Water Supply Map

The Water Supply Map is available from the View Data menu and shows the areas of your city that are watered or unwatered. Areas that are unwanted will show in white.

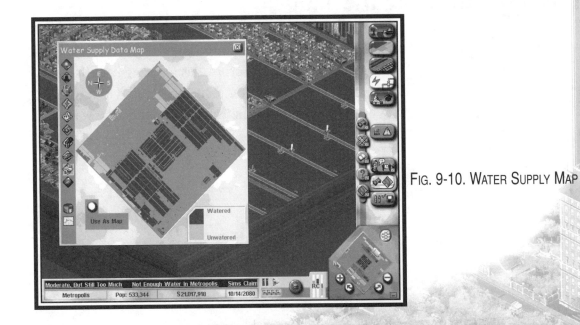

FIG. 9-10. WATER SUPPLY MAP

Water in the Graph Window

Access the city graph from the View Data menu. Check the Water Percent check-box to view your city's water usage over time in the line graph.

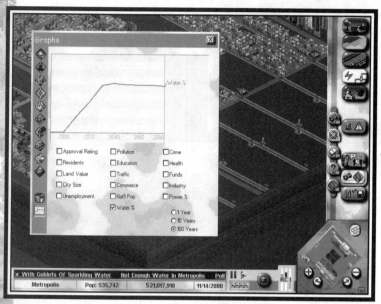

FIG. 9-11. WATER IN GRAPH WINDOW

Placing Water on the Map

You can place water on your City Map anywhere for a minimum cost. This water, as noted in Chapter 6: Land Development and RCI Factors, has a strong beneficial effect on land values. In addition, water placed on the map can be used as a source of pumpable water. Placing a Water Pump next to the water is an effective way to produce more water for your city.

Ordinances

Passing the Water Conservation Ordinance reduces water usage throughout the city by five percent. The Water Conservation Ordinance is available in 1960 and costs §0.0001 per Sim plus one Simoleon for every building in your city. There's an additional side effect in that this ordinance reduces the demand for Industry.

The Mandatory Water Meter Ordinance, available in 1930 and costing §0.0001 per building, also decreases water consumption, in this case, by 10 percent.

Buying and Selling Water

FIG. 9-12. A WATER CONNECTION TO A NEIGHBOR LETS YOU BUY OR SELL WATER.

Building a Water Pipe to the edge of your city presents the opportunity to build a water connection to the neighbor on that side. A water connection costs §2,000. Although you can build as many water connections as you like, only one purchase and one sales deal can exist at any given time, and not to the same neighbor.

For more specifics of how the deals are structured, see chapters 16 and 17.

Pros and Cons of Buying and Selling Water

Assessing the value of a Neighbor Deal requires that you compare the associated costs and benefits of each type of deal. In the case of water, the issues aren't all that complex.

Selling Water Costs

You risk increasing demands and the possibility of having to build more pumping sources, which costs you money and uses up more space.

You risk running out of water pumping capacity and paying a penalty if you default on the deal.

You accept the NIMBY effect of the additional Water Pumps in your city.

Selling Water Benefits

You receive money.

Buying Water Costs

You pay money to receive water.

The money you pay monthly increases over time.

You pay a minimum fee even if you aren't actually using any water from the neighbor.

Buying Water Benefits

You have no NIMBY effect or a reduced NIMBY effect from Pumping Stations.

You save money and space by not having to build Pumping Stations.

Chapter 10
Pollution and Garbage

Once your city really gets going, you'll have to contend with the waste your industry, traffic, and Sims produce. In other words, someone's got to take the garbage out.

There are four major types of pollution that can start adding up in your city. You'll have to deal with keeping your air clean enough to breathe (your Sims don't enjoy bronchitis) and the water safe enough to drink and bathe in without needing to be sterilized beforehand. Garbage can start piling up at an alarming rate, and if you're not careful the streets will soon be overflowing. As time goes on and your city becomes more modern, you may have Nuclear plants in place—and you can't very well ship the radioactive waste (left behind if one of your plants blows up) out into space. Well, not yet, at least.

Pollution is a serious issue in terms of your city's health: the combined pollution rates affect the health and, ultimately, the LE (Life Expectancy) of your Sims. If you've got radiation in addition to air, water, and garbage troubles, the severity of pollutant effects on health and LE will automatically escalate.

Keep your environment clean and healthy! In this chapter, we'll give you the lowdown on the dirty:

- Air pollution
- Water pollution
- Garbage
- Radiation

Pollution is measured in terms of the output of each building, an area of effect, beginning at the edge of the building and decreasing over distance. Normal buildings within zones have a pollution output of 0-125, whereas very heavily polluting buildings can put out as much as 7,000 units of pollution. In addition to building pollution, traffic contributes some air pollution, though air pollution from traffic can be reduced significantly by passing the Car Smogging Ordinance. In any case, air pollution from traffic is not a significant factor when compared with air pollution from buildings.

Calculating Pollution Effects

FIG. 10-1. POLLUTION CAN BUILD UP WHEN MANY POLLUTING BUILDINGS ARE CLUSTERED TOGETHER.

Most buildings in your city will produce some pollution—be it air pollution, water pollution, or just garbage. In the case of air and water pollution, each building has a maximum value of pollution that it generates. This maximum value spreads to a radius of one tile from the building. Each building also has a radius of effect. This is the distance (in tiles) that the pollution from that building travels before reaching zero. As you move farther from any particular building, its pollution effect diminishes, until the radius is reached, at which point its local effect is zero. The actual amount of pollution present on any given tile is based on the pollution effects of multiple buildings and is cumulative. Ultimately, local pollution tends to be cumulative, and when many polluting buildings are clustered together, the effect on surrounding land can be significant—even if each building in the area only produces moderate pollution.

Air Pollution

Your Sims are busy beavers, and the more dams they build, the more sawdust they leave around. Your Sims all live in nice (or not so nice) little houses, and work in Industry or Commercial business—and all buildings in *SimCity* give off a certain amount of air pollution. Traffic also contributes somewhat to the general air pollution level. The amount of air pollution present in your city is measured on a monthly basis. It's calculated as the amount of the monthly pollution output from buildings and traffic density. This level of pollution is then shown in the Air Pollution Map.

FIG. 10-2. USE THE AIR POLLUTION MAP TO IDENTIFY PROBLEM AREAS.

Localized Effects

Air pollution doesn't just spread out and get thinner over the entire city. No way. It tends to hang around the place where it was produced, and this pollution is monitored on a monthly basis. Each building in your city has a maximum pollution value (the amount of pollution generated one tile away) and a radius of effect over which the amount of pollution from that building gradually diminishes to zero. You can see from the Air Pollution Map that certain pockets of a city will have much denser air pollution than others, in large part due to the presence of polluting buildings within a certain radius.

The air pollution resulting from traffic also has a localized effect. As traffic gets more and more dense in one area or another, so too will the air pollution.

FIG. 10-3. ONE WAY TO CUT BACK ON LOCAL POLLUTION BUILD-UP IS TO CREATE SMALLER, DISCRETE INDUSTRIAL ZONES—AND ALONG THE EDGE OF THE MAP WHERE POSSIBLE.

It may be better to create smaller areas of development where pollution will be high. This strategy helps to avoid the cumulative effects of pollution, which will drive land values into the cellar.

Dealing with Air Pollution

What can you do to keep your city's air as clean as you can without forcing the Sims to travel everywhere by bicycle or to go without fireplaces in the winter? There are three main ways to decrease air pollution:

- Place your most polluting buildings near the edge of the map. Effectively, much of the pollution they produce will spread off the map and not affect your city at all.
- Increase the ratio of non-polluting industry to that which pollutes (clean vs. dirty).
- Enact ordinances that promote cleaner air and encourage clean industry.
- Use mass transit to reduce traffic congestion.
- Add occasional nonpolluting elements such as parks or water, which don't add to the cumulative pollution effect.
- Add trees.

Encouraging Clean Industry

Clean or nonpolluting industry becomes more available as time passes. Your city's ratio of clean industry to dirty industry is a factor of your Sims' Education Quotient (EQ) and overall Industrial land values. See the "Demographics" chapter for more information on EQ and its effect on clean industry development, and see Chapter 6: Land Development and RCI Demand for more information on how land values are calculated.

FIG. 10-4. CLEAN INDUSTRY REQUIRES HIGHER EQ, BUT IT'S DEFINITELY WORTH IT. IT'S CLEAN.

Dealing with Traffic

Street traffic causes air pollution. Practically speaking, it's not a major contributor to air pollution, but traffic congestion will cause other serious problems. In general, you want to reduce traffic whenever possible, and the best way to do that is to subsidize mass transit in the form of rails, buses, and subways. When Sims can pile into buses and subways, they'll tend to use their big gas-guzzling cars less often, which helps cut down on the amount of air pollution and keeps your city moving like a well-oiled machine. And don't forget the effects of certain ordinances (see "Air Quality Ordinances"), which can have a significant effect on traffic.

To avoid specific local congestion, alternate routes may be helpful, but remember, once the Sims find a route they like, they tend to use it again and again. Of course, if traffic is very congested in one area and you offer them a less congested way to go, they may take it.

See the "Transportation" chapter for more information about your transit options.

Johnny Appleseed

The effect is very small, but every tree in your city's environment will suck up a small amount of air pollution. There is actually a "Tree Air Factor"—four units of pollution (air and water) for each tile occupied by trees—that tracks this small but green contribution. So, when in doubt, plant a few trees. It can't hurt.

Air Quality Ordinances

There are several ordinances you can enact to help combat the air pollution in your city. Some do so by encouraging clean industry, while others affect other aspects of life in your city:

- Clean Air
- Leaf Burning Ban
- Mandatory Car Smogging
- Landfill Gas Recovery
- Clean Industry Association
- Electronics Tax Incentive
- Aerospace Tax Incentive
- Electronics Job Fair
- Biotech Tax Incentive
- Public Access Cable

Also, traffic-related ordinances affect air pollution because they reduce traffic congestion:

- Parking Fines
- Shuttle Service
- Subsidized Mass Transit
- Alternate Day Driving
- Carpool Incentive

See Chapter 15: Ordinances for more detailed information about each ordinance.

Water Pollution

Water in *SimCity*, like the air, becomes contaminated with pollution over time. In areas of heavy industry, the water turns brownish-black. Each building in your city may produce a certain amount of water pollution—some more than others. In addition, each building has a maximum pollution value (the amount of pollution generated one tile away) and a radius of effect over which the amount of pollution from that building gradually diminishes to zero.

Industrial buildings will tend to produce more polluted water than Commercial or Residential buildings. All that manufacturing just makes more waste, especially if the Industry is high density. High-density areas, in general, will affect the water more intensely than low-density areas.

When water pollution is present in your city, its effect is local, not global. If there is water pollution near your Pumps, Water Towers, and desalinization plants simply won't operate at their maximum efficiency, meaning that some buildings that previously were receiving water might stop getting it. This means higher risk of fire, because unwatered buildings are more flammable. And dehydrated Sims are no fun to deal with.

FIG. 10-5. WATER POLLUTION REDUCES THE EFFECTIVENESS OF WATER STRUCTURES.

How Can You Keep It Clean?

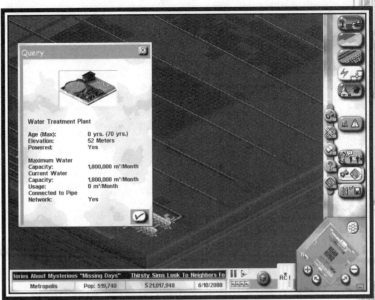

FIG. 10-6. WATER TREATMENT PLANTS ARE THE ONLY WAY TO ELIMINATE WATER POLLUTION.

There's only one way to deal directly with water pollution; you'll need to put in a few Water Treatment Plants, which become available in 1935. These facilities reduce the overall water pollution in your city. The Sims will be cheering in no time—well, actually, the reduction occurs on a monthly basis. Water Treatment Plants cost 15,000 Simoleons each and it's essential that the plant be both powered and connected to the water network. Each Water Treatment Plant can process only 60,000 units of water pollution a month, so determining how many plants you need can be tricky. Your Utilities Advisor will let you know when the situation is really bad, but the other way to tell is to use the Query tool to examine your Water Pumps and Water Treatment Plants. They also show a value for the effect of water pollution. If the pumps are operating at less-than-ideal efficiency or the Water Treatment Plants are operating at their full capacity, then it may be time to consider adding more. As your water starts flowing cleaner, pumps and other machinery in your water system will function better, and the Sims will be opening fire hydrants in their streets to celebrate.

Reducing water polluting buildings is the indirect way to deal with water pollution.

Ordinances

There are two ordinances that will reduce the levels of water pollution in your city:

- Lawn Chemical Ban
- Conservation Corps

For more information and details about these ordinances, including cost and availability, see Chapter 15: Ordinances.

Garbage

Every building in your happy little city produces a certain amount of garbage every month. No doubt the Sims would all prefer that their waste would be magically swept away in the blink of an eye by one Mayoral gesture, but that's not how it is. The monthly garbage output is figured up, for each building, and then begins to pile up if you haven't provided for its disposal.

In simulation terms, there's a difference between garbage—which has to be disposed of, but otherwise has no effect on the city or its Sims—and accumulated garbage, which is considered pollution. Accumulated garbage is any garbage that hasn't been disposed of by one of several means available.

When garbage isn't dealt with, it begins to accumulate. Each building puts out a certain amount of garbage per month, and if this garbage isn't properly disposed of it begins to appear in the filler tiles in zoned areas. If you leave this situation unchecked, pretty soon you've got a real mess on your hands. Garbage-laden filler tiles have a serious effect on land value in their surrounding tiles. A year after the appearance of garbage on landfill tiles, the land value of the surrounding area within the radius of the effect of the landfill is cut in half. Furthermore, the accumulated garbage is considered to be pollution, which means that it gets figured into the overall pollution in your city and will have a negative impact on health and the LE of your Sims.

By the way: Don't even bother trying to bulldoze tiles filled with garbage. It won't work. For some reason, SimBulldozers just can't deal with garbage.

Don't Waste Time Dealing with Waste

Pollution is on the rise. Your Sims are tired of walking around the mountains of garbage in their streets. The overall pollution in your city is increasing. Land values are plummeting, and the LE of your Sims is dropping. What can you do to combat the excessive waste? You've got three tactics to use:

- Garbage disposal
- Garbage reduction
- Neighbor Deal

Reducing the garbage is a helpful measure to take when faced with a mounting waste problem; however, by itself it's not an effective solution. The garbage really needs to be taken out, and there are several ways to do this effectively.

Garbage Disposal Options

There are three garbage disposal methods, each with its costs and benefits, as usual:

- Zone landfill
- Place an incinerator or a waste-to-energy incinerator

Zone Landfill

Fig. 10-8. Landfills will take the waste out of your city, keeping it sparkling clean for your Sims.

Once you've zoned a certain area for a landfill, you're on the way to getting your garbage excess handled in a deep way! At first, when your tiles are zoned appropriately for landfill, you won't see any garbage there. The garbage won't start appearing until the landfill starts accepting it.

Landfill zones don't require power or water, but they do need a minimum zone footprint of 2 × 2. They also require road or rail access so the garbage can be delivered to the zone. You must build a road or rail to at least one edge of the landfill zone for it to be effective. If you're building a rail, you'll need a station at the edge of the landfill. Once it does start, though, you'll see the refuse really pile up. Once a particular landfill tile has reached its maximum amount of garbage, the next one will start to fill up.

Landfills have a very strong NIMBY effect, whether they're full or empty. Because landfills are yucky and gross and unsightly, no one really wants to live near one or develop near one, so you can expect that the land values around your landfill zone will drop considerably. Conclusion? It's a very good idea to place landfill zones as far from other developments as possible.

Garbage gradually decomposes in a landfill, so, assuming that more garbage isn't being heaped on top of it, landfills will eventually become usable for other purposes again if you dezone them. You can't bulldoze a landfill—imagine the grumpy neighbors who'd get covered in rotten fishbones and nasty little bits of old food pushed around by the bulldozers! However, if you do want to reclaim a landfill, you can disconnect it from transportation, then wait for the garbage in it to decompose. This is a slow process; once you stop feeding garbage into a landfill, it will take 25 years for all the garbage to decompose and for the land to become usable again. As long as the landfill remains connected to transportation, and there is garbage to be disposed of, it will continue to accept new garbage if it isn't already full.

Incinerators

FIG. 10-9. INCINERATORS DO GET RID OF GARBAGE, BUT THEY PRODUCE A LOT OF AIR POLLUTION, TOO.

There are two different types of incinerators in *SimCity 3000*: the basic model and the Waste-to-Energy Incinerator. They have certain similarities to each other, in that they both burn garbage and seem to be an easy way to deal with waste management in your city. If you look closer, you'll notice other similarities as well—both kinds of incinerators put out a nasty amount of air pollution. They also have a NIMBY effect on adjacent land values. Hmmm. Maybe this isn't such a quick fix after all.

Incinerators tend to cost more than landfill zones, but they take up less space and can process a larger amount of garbage per tile. The Waste-to-Energy Incinerator is more expensive than the basic incinerator, and actually produces power from the garbage it burns. It generates 70 megawatt hours of power per month, though it needs to be on the power network to provide this power to your city.

Table 10-1 shows comparative information about landfills and the two types of incinerators.

TABLE 10-1. COMPARISON OF GARBAGE DISPOSAL OPTIONS (PER TILE)

Type	Year Available	Garbage Capacity per Day	Cost	Power Supplied
Landfill	Always	variable	50 per tile	0
Incinerator	1920	4500 tons/month	7,500	0
Waste-to-Energy Incinerator	2000	5250 tons/month	25,000	70 MWh

Table 10-2 shows the NIMBY and pollution effects of the three garbage disposal options. The numbers in the table represent modifiers to land value.

TABLE 10-2. NIMBY EFFECTS OF GARBAGE DISPOSAL OPTIONS (PER TILE)

Type	Residential	Commercial	Industrial	All Other	Air Pollution
Landfill	-80	-60	-20	NA	75
Incinerator	-50	-10	-3	-8	4,000
Waste-to-Energy Incinerator	-35	-15	-8	-12	2,500

One way to reduce the negative effects of incinerators is to place them near the edge of the map so that much of their pollution, and even their NIMBY effect, will go off the map and out of your city's hair, so to speak.

There's one more garbage disposal option to consider … .

Neighbor Deals to Export Garbage

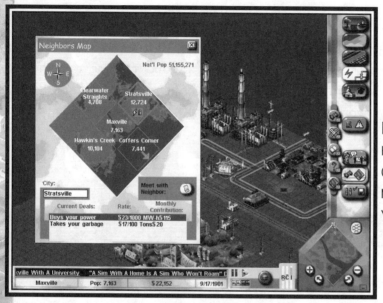

FIG. 10-10. ROAD, RAIL, HIGHWAY, AND SEAPORT CONNECTIONS ALL ALLOW YOU TO MAKE GARBAGE DEALS WITH YOUR NEIGHBORS.

As another creative solution to the piles of garbage in your city, you can strike a garbage deal with any of your neighbors to export your waste to them and have them dispose of it. Although you can only have one garbage export deal at any time (and one import garbage deal, but we'll get to that), you can certainly unload a fair amount of your load onto that neighbor. For a price, of course.

When your accumulated garbage begins to add up and you haven't provided any way to dispose of it yet, *or* if your city is running at 80 percent or higher of its total monthly garbage disposal capacity, you'll get a news ticker message and a Petitioner will soon become available to propose a neighbor deal.

The following are the conditions you must meet to be offered a garbage exporting deal:

- There's a road, highway, rail, or Seaport connection available, and the neighbor to which it's connected isn't already importing or exporting garbage with you through it.

- You're using 80 percent or more of your garbage-handling capacity.
- You aren't currently exporting garbage to any other neighbor.

The Petitioner will list the different terms of the deal, which will be based on a certain rate charged per unit (kiloton) of garbage.

Garbage deals operate on a monthly basis. At the end of each month, the required amount of garbage is exported to the neighbor and the corresponding amount of funds deducted from your treasury. The cost for exporting garbage is based on a given price per kiloton/month. The cost for garbage export typically goes up over time—because your Sims and theirs are competing for the same resource, space in their landfills and incinerators. You're free to accept a deal or reject it—it's completely up to you. If you decide to accept an export garbage deal, the garbage in your city will continue to be disposed of in the facilities you've set up within your city. Once the full capacity of your own waste management network has been reached (just about the time when the Sims get a bit nervous about the possibility of their yards being filled with refuse), the excess garbage will be taken off to your neighbor's city. You'll be charged monthly for the amount of garbage that gets exported in this way, and your budget will be debited. Easy come, easy go.

The rate that you get charged in your garbage export deal is up for review once every five years. You'll see a news ticker indicating that you can renegotiate the terms of your export deal, six months before the rate actually changes. You can meet another Petitioner who'll offer new deal points, and you can accept the deal or reject it during this exchange without penalty. If, however, you just cancel your neighbor garbage export deal at any other time (by using the Neighbor Map or demolishing the connection to the neighbor), your city coffers will be charged a penalty.

To make a garbage export deal with a neighbor, you *must* have:

- No other garbage export deals in place
- No garbage import deal with the same neighbor
- A traditional connection to the neighbor—road, rail, or Seaport

Garbage Import Deals

If you have the capacity to dispose of more garbage than your city produces, then you might want to make a Neighbor Deal that allows you to import your neighbor's garbage and dispose of it. For a fee, of course.

You can be offered a deal (through a Petitioner) to import garbage if the following conditions are met:

- A road, highway, rail, or Seaport is available to a neighbor city and it's not currently being used to import trash.
- You're using 40 percent or less of your garbage-handling capacity.
- You have roads or rails linking the connection point(s) to your landfill(s) and incinerator(s).
- You aren't currently importing garbage from anyone else.
- No other Petitioners are offering to send you their trash.

If you enter into this kind of deal, you'll be required to import a certain amount of garbage from your neighbor each month. Garbage import (and export, for that matter) is calculated in 1,000 ton units (kilotons). The amount imported is determined initially by a number of kilotons multiplied by your neighbor's population, and that amount is updated every five years. The bad news is that if you can't handle the load, both your cities will be inundated with trash—and if it goes on for very long, your neighbor city will cancel the garbage deal and charge you a penalty.

The good news is that you'll also get paid a certain amount each month for the trouble of providing this friendly service for your neighbor. Like the export garbage Neighbor Deal, the import deal will be evaluated and possibly renegotiated every five years. You can decide whether to accept or reject the new terms that are offered.

Your city will be penalized if you fail to dispose of the imported garbage (if you don't have the appropriate landfills or incinerators, etc.) or if you terminate the connection to your neighbor while you have a garbage import Neighbor Deal in place. (You might also want to consult the chapter about Neighbor Deals if you want to get more detailed information about the ins and outs of this process and its overall impact on your city.)

TIP

IF YOU REALLY WANT TO TAKE ON SOMEONE ELSE'S GARBAGE, YOU CAN CONSIDER PLACING INCINERATORS OF VARIOUS KINDS AT THE EDGES OF YOUR MAP. THAT WAY, THE GARBAGE WILL GO DIRECTLY TO THE INCINERATORS, AND THE UNPLEASANT EFFECTS OF THOSE INCINERATORS (POLLUTION AND NIMBY) WILL, AT LEAST PARTIALLY, BE RETURNED TO YOUR NEIGHBOR (OR AT LEAST SENT OFF YOUR CITY'S MAP).

Garbage Reduction Options

There are essentially two methods of reducing the amount of garbage your city produces:

- Recycling centers
- Garbage-reducing ordinances

Recycling Centers

FIG. 10-11. RECYCLING CAN HELP YOU MANAGE YOUR GARBAGE PROBLEM.

Starting in 1970, you can place recycling centers in your city. Recycling centers will effectively reduce garbage output and accumulation on a global basis. One Recycling Center has a maximum effect of reducing overall garbage output by 45 percent, as long as your population doesn't exceed 50,000. If your population grows larger than 50,000 Sims and you only have one Recycling Center, its effectiveness will be seriously diminished, so you'll want to add another Recycling Center for each 50,000 residents in your city. If you keep the ratio of recycling centers at 1:50,000, you'll keep the reduction process functioning smoothly, and the Sims will be more than happy to help out by collecting their old bottles and cans, and hauling them off to the center.

Garbage-Reducing Ordinances

    Industrial Waste Disposal Tax
    Tire Recycling
    Paper Reduction Act
    Backyard Composting
    Trash Presort
    Conservation Corps

    For more information and details, see Chapter 15: Ordinances.
    These six ordinances all help reduce the volume of garbage your city produces. Although each ordinance only becomes an option as time passes, it's a great idea to put one into place (assuming you can afford it) as soon as you find it's available.

Assessment of Garbage Disposal Options

Garbage, garbage, garbage. Just another of those nasty daily realities we all have to come to terms with. Pass your garbage reduction ordinances as soon as you can to help combat the problem.

    It appears that the most effective way of dealing with your garbage in *SimCity 3000* changes as your city develops. Initially, it might serve you well to build a landfill in one corner of the city. It's a fairly cheap, immediate solution to the issue.

    As soon as you can reasonably afford it, though, open a Neighbor Deal (export your trash) and close your landfill by bulldozing road/rail access to it. The trash left behind will decompose in time. Once the land that used to be landfill becomes usable again, you can rezone it again for some other, more productive purpose.

    Incinerators, in the short or long run, just seem more trouble than they're worth. The expense is considerable, and because the incinerators themselves come with a host of horrible NIMBY and pollution effects, they'll probably make your city a mess pretty quickly.

Radiation

FIG. 10-12. IF YOU LET YOUR NUCLEAR PLANT BLOW UP, YOU'VE GOT A BIG PROBLEM.

As your city progresses along in time, the question of having Nuclear power plants will come up. Technological advances make these politically controversial generators available starting in 1960. In *SimCity 3000*, they crank out a whopping 16000 mw-h

Sounds great, doesn't it? Nuclear power plants seem to be the perfect solution to a poor underpowered city's needs. Unfortunately, there is a down side: Just like the other kinds of power plants, nukes can blow up—they will tend to explode if running at over 100 percent capacity. Unlike the other kinds of power plants, when a nuke goes, you can't just bring in the bulldozers to clean up the mess.

If you have a Nuclear power plant that blows up, the consequences are dire for the pollution of your city. When the plant explodes, it scatters radioactive pollution across a 20-tile radius, which is visible to you as little radiation symbols on the affected tiles. The radiation will cause the unfortunate, now-glowing Sims to leave their homes until the radiation effects decay over time (thousands and thousands of years). In other words, in Sim time—never! So much for "duck and cover."

The terrible radiation cloud covers an area of your city and the Sims all desert whatever buildings are in that area. The main effect of this horrible state of affairs (besides a lot of homeless Sims) is that the presence of radiation in your city automatically contributes to the pollution impact on health and LE. What an excess of radiation means, practically speaking, is that it's probably time to quit your current city and start over. Or you can revert to a saved version of the game, pre-nuclear plant explosion, and do what you can to prevent the plant from ruining your city.

On the other hand, if you're into challenges, you can try to keep running your radioactively polluted city … .

Nuclear-Free Zone

Available in 1990 and costing a mere §.00003/Sim, this ordinance not only prohibits the placement of Nuclear power plants and missile silos in your city, it also increases Aura.

In the Case of Nuclear Power Plants

The simple story is that Nuclear plants won't blow up if you don't run them at overcapacity. (Radioactive waste is only a problem if your nuke plant blows up, and then it's pretty much time to start over anyway.) Otherwise, as in *SimCity 2000*, nukes are clean. Nuclear pollution appears not to have any solution—it becomes unbuildable, deserted land in your city.

Ideally, you want to prevent your plants, should you decide to have them at all, from blowing up. For this, we have three short tips:

- Make sure the plants never run at overcapacity, and have disasters turned off *or*
- Have no nuclear power plants at all *or*
- Save your game frequently

Chapter 11
Public Safety

The Sims have moved into new houses, started new jobs, and are settling into their new lives as citizens of your fair city. Once the bare necessities have been taken care of, it's time to consider a new, but familiar, necessity: public safety.

Two aspects of public safety become increasingly important to the residents of your metropolis:

- Fire safety
- Police and jails

Fires are a fairly normal hazard in urban environments. Your Sims do *not* like fire. They want to keep their houses safe and standing. They'd prefer to know that Industrial buildings and Commercial operations will be maintained, and that there'll be no telltale smoke wafting anywhere.

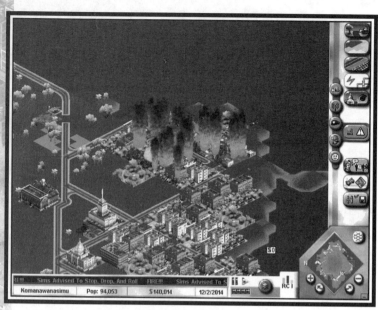

FIG. 11-1. FIRE CAN SPREAD THROUGH A CITY LIKE ... WELL, WILDFIRE.

You'll need to place and fund your Fire Departments. This chapter will describe in detail how to take care of this process to keep the city free of fires, and how to keep yourself from playing with matches.

We'll also talk about how to set up and maintain an effective police force and jail system.

Like most people in cities, the Sims want a safe, crime-free environment. Burglaries, car-jackings, and other urban crimes will need to be kept to a minimum if you're going to keep your city populated with happy Sims. Your police force needs to be funded and maintained appropriately, so that the city's finest are operating at maximum efficiency. You're responsible for placing and funding of police stations and jails, so that Sims are safe to stroll around the streets of your city, secure in the knowledge that theirs neighborhoods are crime free.

Fire Safety

There are two major factors in *SimCity 3000* that contribute to a safe and fire-free city—the placement of Fire Departments and the flammability factor.

Fire Departments

Query

Fire Station

Elevation:	130 Meters
Powered:	No
Watered:	Yes
Number of Fires:	32/Month
Number of Calls:	43/Month
Performance Rating:	Excellent
Spots on Dalmatian:	0
Funding Cost:	§50/Month

FIG. 11-2. PLACE FIRE DEPARTMENTS TO REDUCE THE CHANCE OF YOUR CITY BECOMING AN INFERNO.

Though each Fire Department building is a 3 × 3 structure, every Fire Department protects a certain area around itself that extends far beyond its own structure. This area is referred to as the Fire Protection Radius.

How large and effective the Fire Protection Radius is for a given Fire Department depends on the funding of your Fire Department. The bigger the budget you've allotted to the fearless firefighters, the better their service is and the more area they can cover.

Specifically, each firefighter has an effective radius of 25 tiles at optimum funding, with fire protection being equal over that entire area. Note that this is different from police coverage, which diminishes as the distance from the police station increases. At less-than-optimum funding, the radius of fire protection is reduced accordingly.

The Fire Department is considered to be part of the City Government and needs to be funded as part of the City Budget.

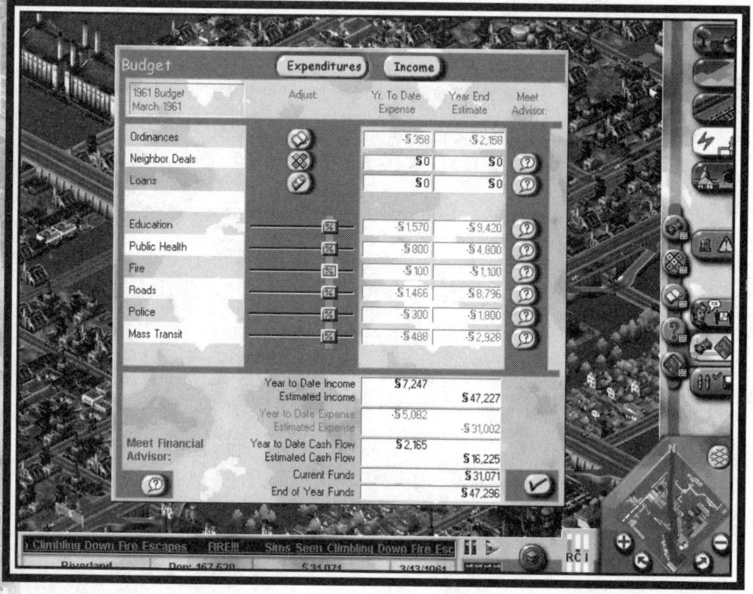

FIG. 11-3. IF YOU'RE WORRIED ABOUT FIRE PROTECTION, THEN YOU'D BETTER SPEND THE MONEY TO KEEP YOUR FIREFIGHTERS HAPPY.

Here are some fire safety facts and figures:

Structure: Fire Department
Footprint: 3 × 3
Fire Protection Radius (when fully funded): 25 tiles in all directions
Cost per month (with 100 percent funding): §30
Emergency Dispatch Icon (sends a squad to the site of a disaster)
Considered part of the City Budget

In Case of Emergency—The Dispatch Icon

FIG. 11-4. PLACE YOUR FIRE-FIGHTERS WHERE THEY'LL DO THE MOST GOOD—RIGHT NEXT TO THE FIRE.

If a fire breaks out beyond a fire protection radius, you must use the Emergency Dispatch Icon. You have one Dispatch Icon for each Fire Department building in your city, plus one for the volunteer fire brigade. For that matter, even within a given Fire Department's operational radius, you can place the Dispatch Icon to hasten the action of firefighting forces.

What this means is that, in case of a disaster or a fire, you can place the Dispatch Icon at the site where a firefighting unit is needed. A faithful asbestos-suited crew will show up, and battle the fire as best it can. Their response time to the fire is immediate. Dispatched firefighters have an effective radius of four tiles. To dispatch firefighters, you just click on the "Emergency" button and select the "Dispatch Firefighters" button. Then, click on the City Map where you want to send them.

No matter how many trucks your department has, however, it'll only have one emergency crew to deploy. (A "bucket brigade," however, is always available by default.) What this means is that, per Fire Department, you can dispatch one emergency unit to the scene of a disastrous fire (so if you've got six Fire Departments, you may have as many as seven emergency units). It's entirely your choice: you can send as many of your available emergency units, or none, if you want, depending on the situation.

Firefighting Strategy

Where there's smoke … there's bound to be fire. Fires may happen, despite your best efforts.

The solutions:

- You can let your Fire Department squads (within the radius of a Fire Department) respond automatically. They'll speed to the scene and start hosing down the flaming buildings.
- If the fire is outside the Fire Protection Radius of any available station, you'll need to dispatch your emergency Dispatch Icon units, as mentioned above.
- Even for fires inside the effective radius of a Fire Department, you can still use the Dispatch Icon to hasten their efforts to put out the blaze.

As a last resort, you can bulldoze tiles around a fire, as a containment effort.

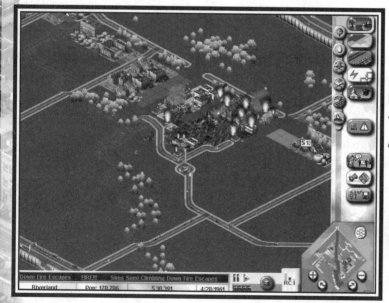

FIG. 11-5. PROPER USE OF YOUR BULLDOZERS CAN MAKE AN EFFECTIVE FIRE BREAK.

NOTE

YOU CAN'T BULLDOZE A TILE THAT'S ACTUALLY ON FIRE. WHAT? YOU WERE THINKING SIMBULLDOZERS AND THEIR OPERATORS WERE FIREPROOF?

If it's fully surrounded by clean, unburnable dirt, a contained fire eventually will burn itself out.

The best way to set up your fire protection—besides turning Disasters off (but that would be cheating, wouldn't it?)—is to make sure that you place enough Fire Departments around your city. You'll want to cover the entire city as best you can, budget permitting. Because the Fire Departments can offer effective protection up to 25 tiles, if you're careful you can overlap protection without wasting money. If you've achieved thorough fire coverage in this way, you may not need to dispatch emergency units at all, because your regularly scheduled Fire Department heroes will save the day.

A word to the wise: Don't place Fire Departments at the edge of your city, because half of the area that department can cover will be outside your city—meaning that it's wasted coverage. Not only that, but you'll still be paying the full price per month for the Fire Department.

Flammability

This is a new feature of *SimCity*. Flammability is effectively a measure of how easily a tile in your city may burn.

Fires can break out anywhere, at any time, in your city. Kids play with matches in a backyard, an industrial accident leads to ignited fuel, and a pile of burning raked leaves gets blown around by the wind. It happens. The *SimCity* simulation "chooses" a random place to start a fire. If that place includes any burnable tiles, a fire may or may not start on one or more of those tiles, depending on the flammability of the tiles.

There are five levels of flammability:

- Low
- Average
- High
- Very High
- Extreme

NOTE

YOU'LL WANT TO TAKE INTO CONSIDERATION, HOWEVER, THE FLAMMABILITY OF THE PARTICULAR AREA THAT'S ON FIRE WHEN DETERMINING WHETHER OR NOT TO DISPATCH FURTHER EMERGENCY TEAMS. FLAMMABILITY IS A NEW FACTOR IN *SIMCITY*, DISCUSSED BELOW.

One way to reduce flammability is to be sure that all your zones are receiving water. Watered buildings are less flammable than unwatered buildings.

If a fire *does* start, how it spreads and grows also depends on the flammability of neighboring tiles. (How quickly a fire can be extinguished depends on the Fire Protection effectiveness of a particular tile.) There are four different stages of growth (intensity) that a fire may go through.

If you don't have resources enough to put out a fire, buildings in your city that are on fire will burn at a rate consistent with their footprint. (In other words, a 1 × 1 house will burn faster than a skyscraper.) If the building tile is consumed completely, the structure explodes. Once it's stopped burning, the flaming tiles leave nothing but a burned-out pile of ashes in their wake—and a number of very unhappy Sims.

Fire Spreading

Once a fire starts, there's a strong likelihood that it'll spread. Any adjacent tile is fair game—especially if it's a burnable tile with a high Inherent Flammability rating. This probability is also determined by the intensity of the fire itself and whatever level of fire protection is in place in that area of your city. Also, if there's a fire on one tile, there's a fair chance that the flames may leap over an unburnable tile to a burnable one and spread there.

Burnable and Unburnable Tiles

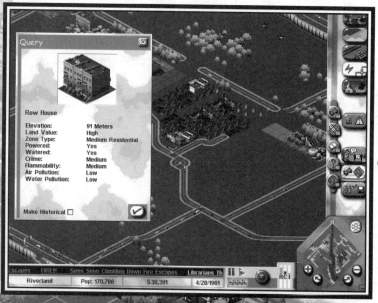

FIG. 11-6. USE THE QUERY TOOL TO CHECK THE FLAMMABILITY OF A BUILDING OR OTHER STRUCTURE.

When you query a burnable tile, you'll see a rating that'll tell you about the Inherent Flammability of that particular tile.

Burnable Tiles:

● All buildings
● All tiles with trees

Unburnable Tiles:

● Roads
● Bare earth
● Rubble
● Water

NOTE

UNDERGROUND LAYER ITEMS LIKE PIPES AND SUBWAYS ARE UNAFFECTED BY FIRES, AS YOU MIGHT IMAGINE.

Caution: Contents of Cities Could Be Highly Flammable

The Fire Protection and Flammability Map, when selected, will show you the status of tiles in your city at any given time. You'll be able to tell which tiles are flammable and how flammable they are, as well as what areas are actually protected by each of your Fire Departments.

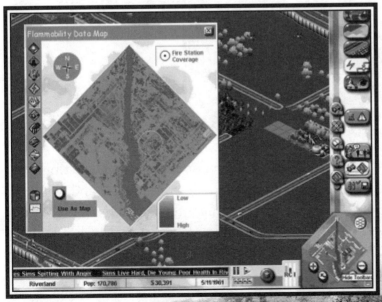

FIG. 11-7.

There are two ordinances that can help keep your city's flammability to a minimum:

TABLE 11-1. FIRE SAFETY ORDINANCES

Ordinance	Year Available	Benefit	Cost
Leaf Burning Ban	1960	-5% flammability	None
Mandatory Smoke Detectors	1970	-10% flammability	§.0001/building

For a more detailed description of these ordinances and their impact on your city, see Chapter 15.

It's also pretty obvious that the lack of water increases flammability. So, to repeat, unwatered sections of your city have an increased flammability level of 25 percent—so make sure those water pipes go everywhere!

Fire Disasters

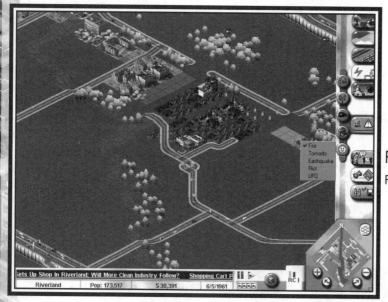

FIG. 11-8. CHOOSE YOUR FAVORITE DISASTER.

Calling all firebugs! If you think the challenge of random fires isn't interesting enough or you simply want to see your buildings burn down to the ground, you can always opt to choose to start fires of your own. The Disasters menu has a fire option. When you select it, a fire will start on some burnable tile in your town. But how can you look your Sims in the eyes after exercising this option?

If you don't want to contend with fire you can turn off disasters—but fire departments will still benefit your aura.

Full Funding for Firefighters

Like other public services, your Fire Departments rely on funding to operate smoothly. Keeping your Sims fire free can get costly. *Not* keeping them fire free can be costlier. You'll want to keep your Fire Departments funded as close to 100 percent as you can to minimize the risk of fire in your city.

Coverage can be increased somewhat through overfunding, to a maximum of 120 percent efficiency However, higher funding doesn't mean an equal increase in protection. That is, a little bit of overfunding will get you a noticeable boost in coverage. More overfunding will increase coverage, but not as much—the maximum efficiency is a point you will never quite reach.

Underfunded Firefighters

If you shortchange the firefighters in your budget, the result could be that the disgruntled heroes go on strike.

If you incur a Fire Department strike:

- Picketers will protest in front of the Fire Department.
- Petitioners representing the employees will appear on the Petitioner List demanding a raise.
- The strike will last for two years (if you do not increase funding), and, if you haven't given in to the firefighters' demands, will end with the workers returning to their jobs.
- Fire Departments will be severely hampered in their effectiveness. Fire protection will be automatically cut in half for the duration of the strike.

Ending a Strike

You have three options for ending a strike, once it has occurred:

● Approve the raise. Everyone will happily go back to work.
● Wait for two years until everyone gives up. Of course, if you continue to keep funding too low, the probability of another strike will continue to increase, starting at the base level for that funding level. Furthermore, your fire hazards will increase, since the effectiveness of the fire crews has been cut in half.
● Demolish every Fire Department, which effectively fires everyone in that department. (Not a highly recommended option.)

Once a strike has ended, the capacity of your Fire Departments will be restored to a level of effectiveness that matches the level to which the departments are funded.

Police Stations

FIG. 11-9. POLICE STATIONS DON'T NEED TO BE CONNECTED TO ROADS, POWER, OR WATER.

The crime levels are rising in your city. Your Sims are disgruntled and frightened. If you don't do something, and quickly, you'll start to lose population. What can you do? It's time to put your city's finest out on the streets to fight crime.

Police are your tools for fighting crime in the neighborhoods of your city. Use them as needed. Jails, discussed a bit later, are buildings at the city level that also help, along with the police force, to reduce crime.

Police stations in *SimCity 3000* function like Fire Departments in several respects:

Structure: police station
Footprint: 3 × 3
Protection Radius (when fully funded): 30 tiles in all directions
Cost per month (funded 100 percent): §30
Emergency Dispatch Icon (sends a squad to the site of a disaster)
Considered part of the City Budget

About the Station

Each police station is a structure that occupies a 3 × 3-tile footprint in your city, providing a radius of police protection around the structure. This radius, when the Station is fully funded, will extend as much as 30 tiles in all directions around a given station. What this means is that crime levels within this radius will be considerably reduced, as compared to areas in your city that are *not* covered by a police station.

FIG. 11-10. POLICE STATIONS HAVE A RADIUS OF EFFECT THAT DEPENDS ON THE LEVEL OF FUNDING.

As with Fire Departments, the police station's radius of coverage and effectiveness of coverage depends on their budget. How much you fund the Station determines how many cops you'll get and how diligent those men in blue really are when they're on the beat. However, coverage is highest close to the police station and will fall off in a linear fashion until it reaches zero at the edge of that station's coverage radius.

Police stations placed near each other will provide overlapping police protection for a given area, assuming they're well funded. The Sims in your city will appreciate the extra presence of the officers where the influences of different stations overlap. The police effectiveness in overlapping areas is equal to the sum of the overlapping areas. For example, if the outermost level of police coverage by one station is 20 and you drop another station so its outermost area (also at 20) overlaps this, the actual coverage in that area is 40. In high-crime areas, it's a good idea to provide some overlapping coverage to offset the diminishing effect of police coverage over distance from the station. Too much police coverage will lower aura because it is oppressive.

FIG. 11-11. PLACING POLICE STATIONS NEAR EACH OTHER CAUSES THEIR INFLUENCE TO OVERLAP, WITH A RESULTING INCREASE IN EFFECTIVENESS.

In Case of Emergency or Riots

Your police force is especially handy in an emergency situation. Like the Fire Departments, each police station has an emergency dispatch unit in case of true disasters. You can move the Dispatch Icon to the scene of the crime and a unit of officers will be sent promptly.

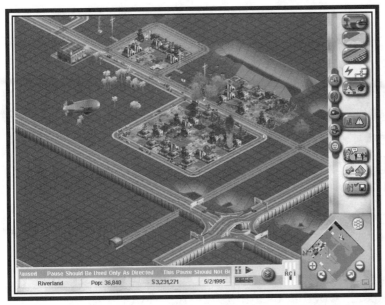

Fig. 11-12. Police are most effective during riots.

Again, similar to the way Fire Departments operate, if you've placed your police stations effectively around your city (and they're well funded), you probably won't need to use the Dispatch Icon. But it's nice to know it's there, just in case, especially if a disaster of epic proportions hits your city and you find yourself a little short-handed in the police station.

The Crime Layer

The Crime Layer is the way that *SimCity* measures how much crime is going on in your city at any given time. What most affects the Crime Layer is the RCI layer, interestingly enough. Every RCI building type in your city has a particular amount of crime that corresponds to the building. Certain types of buildings that you can choose to place in the city, like Stadiums and Casinos, also have particular crime values.

If your city legalizes gambling, for instance, the crime rate in the area around a Casino will increase considerably. Crime in general can be reduced by using the three following methods:

- Passing ordinances
- Improving property values
- Placing enough police stations

Ordinances and Crime

TABLE 11-2: CRIME ORDINANCES

Ordinance	Available	Benefit	Cost
Youth Curfew	Always	Reduces crime, increases youth EQ	§0.0001/Sim+ # of police stations
Junior Sports	Always	Reduces crime, increases youth EQ	§0.00007/Sim
Neighborhood Watch	1970	Reduces crime citywide	§0.000055/Sim
Legalized Gambling	Always	Increases crime	Raises 0.001/Sim

For an in-depth discussion of these ordinances and their effects, see Chapter 15.

You'll notice that the Legalized Gambling Ordinance actually *increases* crime in your city. It's up to you to decide whether a casino's revenue is worth it.

Police and the Crime Layer

Your police force works hand-in-glove with the Crime Layer of your city and the relationship is demonstrated in two major ways.

Crime reduction for any given tile is subtracted from the crime value for that particular tile. This means that the crime value for a particular building or area of buildings is affected by the effectiveness of your police coverage. If you query your police station, you can check the ratio of policemen to crimes in the area. Under the best circumstances, the number of officers will be greater than the number of crimes that are committed. If this *isn't* the case, you might want to consider adding other police stations or making sure that your existing station has a high enough budget allotment to keep the officers operating at the highest level of effectiveness.

FIG. 11-13. USE THE QUERY TOOL ON A POLICE STATION TO SEE HOW EFFECTIVE IT IS AT STOPPING CRIME.

Property values are enhanced by the presence of police stations. Remember, if crime in a local area is less than a set value, that area receives a positive land value effect. If crime is zero, then the area is sure to receive some benefit. And higher land value ultimately results in higher tax revenue … and we like that, don't we?

This is a great relationship, because when you place a police station in a given area, the property values automatically increase. When the values rise, the RCI buildings in the area are affected. This extra wealth and land value actually further reduce crime in the neighborhood! Instead of the old "NIMBY" blues, the Sims in potential police station neighborhoods are singing the "YIMBY" refrain—the Yes, In My Back Yard song.

Well-Funded Police Stations

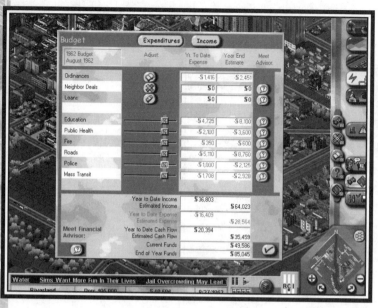

FIG. 11-14. KEEP YOUR CRIME FIGHTERS HAPPY. DON'T UNDERFUND POLICE.

A police station that's fully funded will provide optimum crime protection coverage for the 30-tile radius surrounding the station. There's little point in overfunding because the resulting increase in protection won't be much higher.

Also, if you *seriously* overfund your police station, you run the risk of developing a super-powered, repressive police force. If the protection becomes oppressive, the Aura of your city will be impacted negatively—and a riot could result. However, if you still want to do this, police coverage can be increased somewhat through overfunding, to a maximum of 120 percent efficiency. As with your Fire Department, a little bit of overfunding will get you a noticeable boost in coverage. Even more overfunding will increase coverage, but not as much—so you encounter diminishing returns as you increase funding above 100 percent.

Underfunding the Fuzz

If you neglect to fund the police station, it's likely that the officers will go on strike.
If you should incur a police station strike:

Picketers will protest in front of the police station.
Petitioners representing the employees will appear on the Petitioner List demanding a raise.
The strike will last for two years (unless you increase funding to 100%), and, if you have done nothing, will end with the workers returning to their jobs.
Your city will behave as if the police are severely hampered in their effectiveness.
Crime protection will be automatically cut in half for the duration of the strike.

Ending a Strike

You have three options for ending a strike, once it has occurred:

● Approve the raise. Everyone will happily go back to work.
Wait for two years, when everyone gives up. Of course, if you continue to keep funding too low, the probability of another strike will continue to increase, starting at the base level for that funding level. Furthermore, your crime rate will sky-rocket, since the effectiveness of your police force has been cut in half.
Demolish every police station, which effectively fires everyone in that department. (Not a highly recommended option.)

Once a strike has ended, the capacity of your police station will be restored to a level of effectiveness that matches the level to which the stations are funded.

Jails

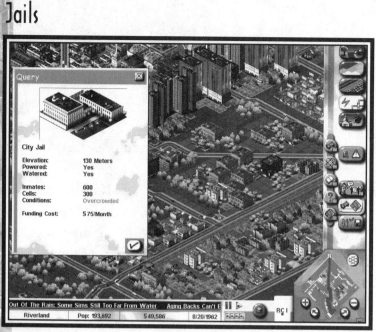

Query

City Jail

Elevation: 130 Meters
Powered: Yes
Watered: Yes

Inmates: 600
Cells: 300
Conditions: Overcrowded

Funding Cost: $75/Month

Fig. 11-15. Jails can increase the effectiveness of your police stations.

Out Of The Rain: Some Sims Still Too Far From Water   Aging Backs Can't E
Riverland   Pop: 193,692 $ 49,586   8/20/1962

The presence of a jail can increase the effectiveness of your police stations significantly. A city without jails suffers a 25 percent reduction in the efficiency of its police force.

If the police station is more effective, then the crime value of tiles in the area surrounding the station will be diminished. By the same token, if you lack a jail within the radius of police protection, the crime value of local tiles may increase.

Throughout your city, jails are an unfortunate necessity in the battle against crime. Jails operate in conjunction with the police station system to increase the effectiveness of your police force. Although they're not pretty to look at, jails are a great help in reducing crime in your city.

The need for a jail is based on the ratio of the number of inmates to the number of available jail cells (in the entire city):

Table 11-3. Jail Cells and Police Effectiveness

Number of Inmates	Police Effectiveness
Less than number of available cells	Increase of 25%
Greater than number of available cells by 1%–10%	Increase of 25%
Greater than number of available cells by 10% or more	Increase is reduced in proportion to number of inmates to cells over 110%

Chapter 12
Meet the Sims, Meet Their Needs

The Sims are the tiny computer people who populate your city. Like citizens everywhere, they have particular needs and preferences about how the city ought to operate. If these needs aren't met effectively, you may wind up as the mayor of a ghost town.

In terms of demographics, your city is filled with people who correspond to a particular Age Distribution, Life Expectancy (LE), and Education Quotient (EQ). These different factors all contribute to the strength of your city's workforce and the way that Industrial development occurs.

The Sims are born, they age and grow, and then die, just like real people. The ages of your Sims are significant, because Sims between the ages of 20 and 55 represent your workforce. This is the responsible, adult population who're holding down jobs, and as such, they directly affect Commercial and Industrial growth/health in your city. So, you want to ensure that you've got healthy, happy Sims—and lots of them— getting old enough fast enough to fill these jobs.

The Education Quotient, or EQ, has a particularly significant impact—the higher the EQ of your Sims overall, the more likely your city is to have clean industry. (And you know that those high-polluting Industrial areas will only lead to a dead end, don't you?)

Improving the quality of life for your Sims has a direct impact on their Life Expectancy, or LE. Many factors contribute to the decay of Sims over time: pollution rates, a weak health network (not enough hospitals), and a lack of public ordinances. Sims who have an improved LE will result in higher numbers of Sims in the workforce, in offspring with higher EQs, and ultimately in a city where clean industry prevails.

So now you know how important your Sims' ages, Life Expectancy, and Educational Quotient really are. What can you do to keep the optimum number of Sims between the ages of 20 and 55? What can you do to help SimJohnny read and raise the overall EQ of your city? And how can you best keep those Sims leading happy, healthy, longer lives?

You'll find these answers in this chapter, where we'll discuss:

- Population
- Age Distribution
- Education Quotient (EQ)
- Life Expectancy (LE)

A Word about Population

Your city starts off with some Sims moving in from who knows where. They've brought you the proud, the hungry, the tired. Most of these Simmigrants are in the working-age range (20 to 55 years old). Initially, the only way your city will gain population is by Simmigration like this. Residential zones will take off as Sims move in, clean house, plant flowers, and sweep their little sidewalks free of SimDirt.

Age Distribution

Once your Residential zones start serious development, each building that appears has a certain number of Sims living in it. A population number is assigned, per building, and will differ from building to building. The populated Residential buildings, taken together, form your city's total population at any given time. This figure is then broken up into the ages of your Sims, and forms the Age Distribution of your city.

When tracking ages, the Sims are divided into 19 major groups, from birth to a maximum Life Expectancy (LE) of 90. These groups are based on five-year age increments (for example, ages 0–5, 6–10, and so on). Basically, though, you have young children, children, college-age young people, the workforce (between 20 and 55 years old), and the retired Sims.

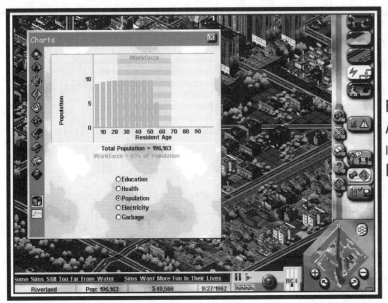

FIG. 12-1. YOU CAN SEE THE AGE DISTRIBUTION OF THE SIMS IN YOUR CITY BY CHECKING THE POPULATION BAR.

Education Quotient

The Education Quotient, or EQ, of your population is incredibly significant and, in fact, contributes greatly to one of the primary goals of your city. Over time, if your population raises its EQ considerably, the amount of clean industry that you have will also rise. Your city can't support advanced industry that pays well and leaves little waste in its wake unless the EQ of your population starts climbing toward that maximum EQ of 150. This is especially important in your city's later stages, when the demand for clean industry increases. EQ is also one of the values used in calculating your city's Aura.

Every Sim has an initial EQ that's determined at birth. This EQ number is arrived at by dividing the average EQ of all the working-age Sims in your city by five. When you launch a new city, the average EQ of your workforce is 58. This number reflects the equivalent of a high school education. Given that the average United States EQ is modeled around 100, and the maximum possible EQ in *SimCity* is 150, you've got your work cut out for you.

Within each five-year age division, the EQ of that segment of the overall population is evaluated and the EQ is then raised or lowered, as determined by factors in your city's development (like how many schools, colleges, and Libraries are in place). The workforce EQ average will rise or fall according to these evaluations, as will the EQ set at birth. Over the course of the first 15 years of life, Sims generally acquire 4/5 of their parents' EQ or 120 EQ points, whichever is smaller. These are considered to be the parent-aged Sims. In time, your population's EQ will rise if you're providing your city with the appropriate building blocks.

After age 25, Sims begin to experience EQ decay, unless Libraries and other facilities are put in place to allow them to continue their educational path of discovery and stave off the effects of EQ entropy.

How To Raise the Education Quotient

FIG. 12-2. YOUR SIMS START OUT AT A PRETTY LOW EQ.

FIG. 12-3. IF YOU GIVE THEM WHAT THEY NEED, THEY'LL GET SMARTER.

At first, you'll want to create schools to educate the young Sims. Lower schools in *SimCity 2000* could handle a maximum of 1,500 students, or an overall population of about 15,000. Schools can be infinitely overcrowded; funding doesn't affect capacity. It only affects the amount of EQ delegated to each Sim. Their initial EQ, for ages zero to five, is set at birth. To achieve the maximum increase, there must be enough well-funded schools and colleges so that each Sim child gets a full education.

FIG. 12-4. SCHOOL IS WHERE SIMS GET SMARTER.

Specifically, Kindergarten through twelfth grade schools improve the EQ of Sims aged 6 through 18, while colleges help those aged 19 to 24. Although the increments in EQ reported to you by your advisor are at five-year increments, the simulation itself actually tracks EQ on a yearly basis.

To get the most out of *SimCity 3000*, the population between the ages of 6 and 24 years old needs to be in school. If this goal is met, the overall EQ of your population will rise. For our purposes, we'll assume that approximately 10 percent of the population is at school age. Therefore, if a school can support 3,000 students, you need one school for every 30,000 Sims to have 100 percent of your school-aged Sims educated. The following factors are associated with schools:

TIP

SCHOOLS ARE IMPORTANT, BUT THEY ALSO COST MONEY TO BUILD AND TO MAINTAIN. SO, YOU MAY NOT WANT TO GO HOG WILD AND BUILD ANY SCHOOLS UNTIL YOUR CITY'S POPULATION IS AT LEAST ABOVE 20,000.

● Capacity (a fixed number) = 3,000

- Students = the total number of Sims between ages 6 and 18
- Teachers = base number of teachers modified by funding
- Performance Rating = the student-to-teacher ratio, expressed as a grade (A to F)
- Optimal Monthly Upkeep = §30, the amount required each month to keep a school running at optimal capacity

Schools have a limited capacity for students. A school system's effectiveness is expressed as a grade (from A+ to F) and is based on the percentage of available students who aren't served by the school and by the student-to-teacher ratio of the schools in the system. Student-to-teacher ratios are determined by the amount of funding you give your school system. The school's grade essentially reflects that school's effectiveness at raising the EQ of your population, and of course you'll want to do what you can to get straight A pluses whenever possible.

FIG. 12-5. TO GET THE HIGHEST EQ, MAKE SURE YOU PROVIDE COLLEGES FOR YOUR SIMS.

Hopefully you'll have planned ahead to provide for your high school graduates' futures by providing them with colleges by the time they're ready to move on. Colleges have a direct impact on the EQ of Sims between the ages of 19 and 24 years old, and will yield (again, under optimum conditions) an EQ value per Sim that is one and one-half times the EQ the Sim has upon entering college. For our purposes, we'll assume that approximately 10 percent of the population is college age. Therefore, if a college can support 7500 students, you need one college for every 150,000 Sims to be 100 percent effective. The following factors are associated with colleges:

- Capacity (a fixed number) = 7500
- Attendance = the total number of Sims between ages 19 and 24
- Teachers = fixed number per college modified by funding
- Performance Rating = the student-to-teacher ratio, expressed as a grade (A to F)
- Optimal Monthly Upkeep = §125, the amount required each month to keep a college running at optimal capacity

Lack of Funding for Schools and Colleges

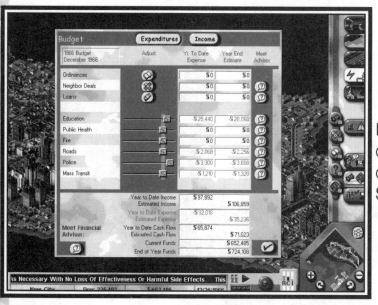

FIG. 12-6. YOU GET THE MOST OUT OF YOUR SCHOOLS IF YOU GIVE THEM PLENTY OF SIMOLEONS.

When there's not enough money pouring into your schools and colleges, you've got real headaches on the way. Schools that are underfunded will become much less effective overall. The effect of floundering schools is that the teachers, underpaid and overworked already, may decide they've simply had enough and go on strike. Schools will not affect the EQ of your Sims in a beneficial way while the teachers are striking—in fact, the EQ will plummet.

If you find yourself with a strike on your hands, the following will occur:

Picketers will protest in front of the schools and colleges.

Petitioners representing the employees will appear on the Petitioner List demanding a raise.

The strike will last for two years (unless you increase funding) and, if you've done nothing, will end with the workers returning to their jobs.

Your city will behave as if educational services don't exist. This, in turn, will affect EQ drastically.

Ending a Strike

You have three options for ending a strike once it has occurred:

Approve the raise or increase funding to 100%. Everyone will happily go back to work.

Wait for two years until everyone gives up. Of course, if you continue to keep funding too low, the probability of another strike will continue to increase, starting at the base level for that funding level.

Demolish every school, or college, which effectively fires everyone in education.

Obviously, the last option is pretty drastic and probably less desirable than just giving out the raise or waiting the two years. Once the schools are back in operation, however, it would behoove you to restore funding to full levels as soon as you can; otherwise you'll soon have another strike on your hands.

EQ Can Decay (If You Don't Brush Regularly)!

Just like in real life, once the Sims stop going to school or attending college, they tend to forget the majority of what they've learned. Their EQs start falling and will continue to do so as they age. This is expressed in *SimCity 3000* as a decay in the EQ of your city's population.

As long as your Sims get a regular brush with culture at institutions where they can keep learning after college, your EQ won't fall off. There are two ways to prevent EQ decay:

- Placing culturally stimulating buildings
- Passing the Pro-Reading Campaign Ordinance

Buildings

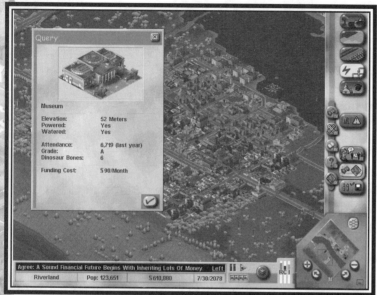

FIG. 12-7. LIKE LIBRARIES, MUSEUMS CAN HELP KEEP YOUR SIMS AT THEIR MAXIMUM EQ EVEN AFTER THEY LEAVE SCHOOL.

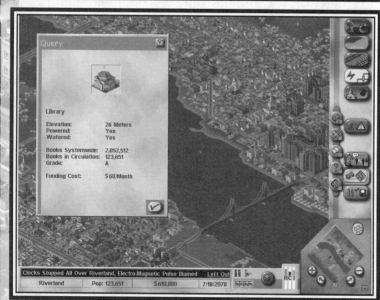

FIG. 12-8. LIBRARIES HELP KEEP YOUR SIMS SHARP AND ON THE BALL.

If you place Libraries and Museums in your city, you can counteract the effects of EQ decay. Each Library will slow the EQ decay of a maximum of 41,000 Sims. Museums will affect a maximum population of 83,000. The effectiveness of these facilities on EQ decay will be reduced if the population exceeds the maximum numbers, and you'll need to build another Library or Museum.

Ordinances

Passing certain ordinances will help boost EQ and can sometimes combat EQ decay.

TABLE 12-1: EQ ORDINANCES

Ordinance	Cost
Pro-Reading	§.0000125/Sim + the cost of libraries
Junior Sports	§0.00007/Sim
Youth Curfew	§0.0001/Sim

Life Expectancy (LE)

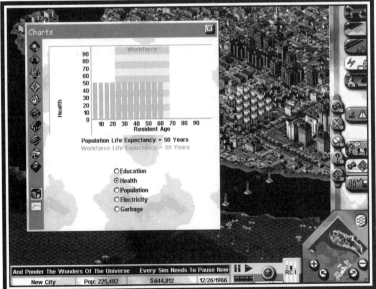

FIG. 12-9. HOW LONG WILL YOUR SIMS LIVE?

How healthy are your Sims? Life Expectancy, or LE, is set at the time a SimBaby is born and serves as an indicator of health. When your city's just beginning, the average LE of a baby Sim is around 59 to 65 years. This isn't the greatest, since you want to encourage your Sims to have long, happy, healthy lives so that they'll stay in the workforce longer and produce new Sims with longer LEs who'll stay in the workforce longer and so on. (The higher the LE, the more Sims are actually in your workforce.) Over time, the average LE can be raised to a maximum of 90 years, but it'll take time and many generations.

Why would you want your Sims living long lives? Your city's Aura increases if your Sims are living longer, happier lives.

If people are going to live long lives in your city, you'll have to be vigilant about maintaining their EQ levels—and putting in Libraries and Museums and so on could get pretty costly.

LE also affects EQ (Education Quotient) in a clear way. If your Sims are dying too young, it means they won't have enough of a chance to raise their EQ. You definitely want to have clever Sims in the workplace; it's all that much more efficient and the repartee is better. Not to mention the obvious impact on clean Industrial development.

LE Decay

LE can be impacted negatively by several factors in your city's development. Like EQ, LE can decay over time if the environment isn't geared to prevent this decay. LE is affected over time by pollution, smoking, and the absence of enough fully funded hospitals. The more polluted your city gets or the fewer hospitals there are, the more the LE of your Sims will drop. You really don't want this to happen, because the Sims get pretty cranky as they get sick and start dying too young.

So what can you do to prolong Sim lives and keep them healthy? There are three main tools for raising LE in *SimCity*:

- Building and funding hospitals
- Passing ordinances
- Improving the quality of life
- Promoting clean industry
- Reducing pollution

Hospitals

FIG. 12-10. HOSPITALS HELP KEEP YOUR SIMS HEALTHY SO THEY CAN LIVE LONGER LIVES.

The first step is to make sure you've got enough fully funded hospitals in town. Because SimBabies are assigned their LE at birth, you'll want to increase the chances of healthy births so that the newborns have a good chance to see that 90-year maximum LE. The following factors are associated with hospitals:

- Capacity (a fixed number) = 1500
- Number of patients = based on the percentage of the population that is sick divided by the total capacity of hospitals in the city. The percentage of the population that is sick starts at five percent but can rise with pollution; therefore, you'll need more hospitals as the city becomes more polluted.
- Doctors = percentage of total population times the percentage of hospital funding
- Performance Rating = the doctor-to-patient ratio, expressed as a grade (A to F)
- Optimal Monthly Upkeep = §50 per hospital

Funding Hospitals

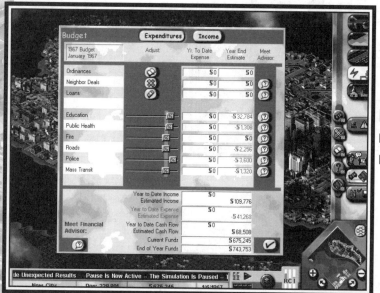

FIG. 12-11. FOR HOSPITALS TO BE EFFECTIVE, THEY MUST RECEIVE ADEQUATE FUNDING.

You'll want to keep your hospitals as well funded as you can. Underfunded hospitals mean that you're running the risk of the hospital staff going on strike.

If you should incur a hospital strike:

Picketers will protest in front of the hospital.

Petitioners representing the employees will appear on the Petitioner List demanding a raise.

The strike will last for two years (unless you increase funding to 100%) and, if you've done nothing, will end with the workers returning to their jobs.

Your city will behave as if hospital service doesn't exist. This, in turn, will affect LE.

Ending a Strike

You have three options for ending a strike once it has occurred:

Approve the raise. Everyone will happily go back to work.

Wait for two years until everyone gives up. Of course, if you continue to keep funding too low, the probability of another strike will continue to increase, starting at the base level for that funding level.

Demolish every hospital, which effectively fires all the employees.

Obviously, the last option is pretty drastic and probably less desirable than just giving out the raise or waiting the two years. Once the hospitals are operating again, however, you should restore funding to full levels as soon as you can; otherwise you'll soon have another strike on your hands.

Ordinances

Several ordinances can have a positive effect on your population's LE: Free Clinics Ordinance, the Public Smoking Ban Ordinance, and the CPR Training Ordinance. For more information about these ordinances, see Chapter 15.

TABLE 12-2. LE ORDINANCES

Name	Cost
Free Clinics	§0.0001/Sim
Community CPR Training	§0.00003/Sim
Public Smoking Ban	§0.0006/Sim
Crossing Guards	§0.0005/Sim

Other Measures

Make the quality of life in SimCity better by cutting back on pollution from industry and traffic, cleaning up garbage, etc. Garbage in landfills won't adversely affect your Sims' health, but garbage that accumulates in the city has a detrimental effect. If the environment is healthy, your Sims will be, too. Remember, what's bad for your Sims is bad for your city, and what's bad for your city is bad for your career.

Chapter 13
City Aura
Mayor Rating

City Aura is an expression of how your Sims feel about their city, their "civic pride" so to speak. This Aura translates into a mayoral rating and is figured by combining various factors about quality of life—rather like the way in which U.S. cities are rated annually for their desirability as a place to live. These factors include the relative levels of pollution, education, health, crime, and other issues.

There is both a Local Aura—which translates into good versus bad neighborhoods—and Global Aura—which serves as a mayoral rating. That way you always know the answer to the question, "How am I doin'?"

Local Aura

TIP

SIMCITY 2000 ONLY USED THE MAYOR RATING AS AN INDICATOR OF HOW SIMS FELT. KIND OF LIKE A DOCTOR TAKING A PATIENT'S TEMPERATURE, IT COULD TELL YOU IF YOUR CITY WAS WELL AND THRIVING OR SICK AND FAILING, BUT THE RATING COULDN'T REALLY TELL YOU MUCH MORE. IN SIMCITY 3000, YOU CAN USE AURA NOT ONLY FOR THE OVERALL RATING OF YOUR ENLIGHTENED MAYORAL RULE, BUT ALSO TO IDENTIFY SPECIFIC PROBLEM AREAS OF CIVIC PRIDE. WHEN YOU IDENTIFY A PROBLEM AREA OR LOCATION IN YOUR CITY, YOU CAN TAKE STEPS TO MAKE YOUR SIMS FEEL BETTER ABOUT THEIR SITUATION.

Have you ever visited an area of a city and said, "Oh, what I wouldn't give to live here!" Or, conversely, "Goodness, what a rat hole!" Well, many of the same factors that differentiate between "Wow!" and "Blech!" go into determining the Local Aura.

In *SimCity 3000*, Local Aura is calculated by considering:

- Police coverage and effectiveness: inadequate, sufficient, or oppressive, as well as crime rates
- Fire coverage
- Local building effects: NIMBY, YIMBY
- Pollution: air, water, garbage, and noise

Police and Crime

Your Sims are very particular about law-and-order issues, making your job as Mayor a real balancing act. Sims want enough police coverage so they don't have to install burglar bars on their homes and apply for concealed weapons permits. On the other hand, they don't want cops strutting around like jackbooted thugs, intruding on their civil rights.

Just like Goldilocks and the Three Bears, what you're striving for is police coverage that is "just right," neither too much nor too little.

TABLE 13-1. EFFECTS OF POLICE COVERAGE ON AURA

Factor	Effect
High crime rate	Lower Aura
Inadequate police coverage	Lower Aura
Optimal police coverage	Higher Aura
Oppressive police coverage	Lower Aura

Fire Coverage

There's apparently no such thing as being too safe from fires. As long as your Sims feel reasonably secure about the fire safety of their homes and workplaces, they're happy. Sufficient and optimal fire coverage results in a positive effect on local Aura. Insufficient coverage merely foregoes that positive influence. Excessive fire department coverage just throws money away and gives your city's firefighters a little too much time on their hands and encourages them to drive their underutilized fire trucks in every parade.

Building Effects

Aura can be influenced by the presence of certain buildings or structures. Again, using the "good" versus "bad" neighborhood, this is pretty easy to understand just by comparing how you might imagine feeling during a cocktail party when someone asks, "So where do you live?"

People with high auras take pride in their houses situated near the Performing Arts Center and the Public Library, whereas low-aura Sims are ashamed of their run-down, polluted neighborhoods.

The following table shows the local effects of specific buildings and structures, as well as their radius of influence:

TABLE 13-2. NIMBY EFFECTS ON AURA

Building/Structure/Zone	Relative Aura Effect Radius	Effect on Aura
Low-density dirty Industry	0	-1
Medium-density dirty Industry	0	-2
High-density dirty Industry	0	-3
Power plant (variable)	-1	1
Bus station	4	-1
Rail station	8	-2
Parking lot	1	-1
Airport	0	-2
Seaport	0	-2
Pile of garbage	8	-6
Water sewage	8	-2
Water Pump	1	-1
Water Tower	1	-1
Penal institution (jail, prison)	20	-3
LD Dirty Ind	0	-1
MD Dirty Ind	0	-2
HD Dirty Ind	0	-3
Microwave Power Plant	15	-2
Nuclear Power Plant	20	-3
Fusion Power Plant	10	-1
Garbage	8	-6
Space Port	10	-2
City Jail	15	-2

TABLE 13-3. YIMBY EFFECTS ON AURA

Building/Structure/Zone	Relative Aura Effect Radius	Effect on Aura
Agriculture (farm)	4	2
Hospital	15	2
Library	15	2
Museum	20	1
Statue, fountain	15	1
Historic building	8	1
Park	8	2
Marina	15	2
Zoo	20	1
Stadium	20	2
City Hall	20	3
Medical Research Center	15	2
Performing Arts Center	20	3
Lighthouse	15	2
Flora	1	1
Stock Exchange	15	1
Mayor's House	10	2
Military Base	20	1
University	20	1
City College	10	2
Geyser Park	20	1
Theme Park Puzzle Zone	15	1

Pollution and Aura

Local pollution has a strong negative effect on Aura. Seems obvious, but Sims (just like real people) just don't like being near air or water pollution or having to pass by piles of garbage. They're funny that way. Anyhow, the higher the local pollution levels, the greater the negative impact on local Aura.

The following are things Sims just don't like:

- Air pollution
- Water pollution
- Standing piles of smelly garbage
- Radioactive fallout

Global Aura

Global Aura is determined by averaging Local Aura across your entire city, then modifying it by the effects of certain factors that add or subtract to the desirability of living there in general. These include:

- Ordinances (both positive and negative)
- Education (high or low average, and whether it is rising or falling)
- Health (high or low, and whether it is improving or failing)

A high Global Aura (which equals a high mayoral rating) results in various messages mentioning how wonderful you are. A low Global Aura can result in Sims demanding you change certain ordinances or policies.

Ordinances

Some ordinances have a direct influence in making your Sims happier, others make them irate.

Positive Aura ordinances:

Nuclear Free Zone Ordinance

Negative Aura ordinances:

- Parking Fines
- Alternate Day Driving

Education and Health

These are fairly easy to figure. High Education Quotients (EQs) and Life Expectancies (LEs) result in a positive boost to Global Aura. And, of course, low EQs or LEs reduce Global Aura.

Aura Displays

Aura is displayed in the Aura Data Map, or in City View, if that option is selected. The map shows a spectrum from good to bad Aura, with lines and graphics to represent roads and such to help orient you.

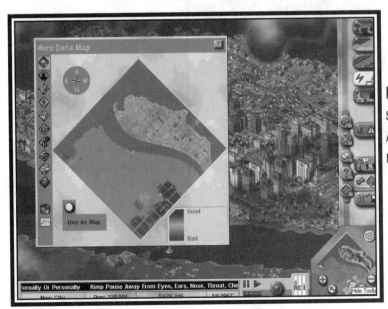

FIG. 13-1. AURA IS ONE WAY TO SEE JUST HOW HAPPY YOUR SIMS ARE WITH YOUR ENLIGHTENED MAYORAL RULE.

Want some specifics? There are some places where you can get a more, ahem, graphic demonstration of how happy your Sims are with your rule as Mayor:

- The Mayor's House: the number of eggs thrown at your house is zero when your Aura is high (upper 10 percent of range), and can be from 1 to 99 if the Aura is less than high
- Historic Statue: the number of pigeons hanging around the statue erected in your honor

Another way you can get a look at your approval rating is in the charts section of the View Data display.

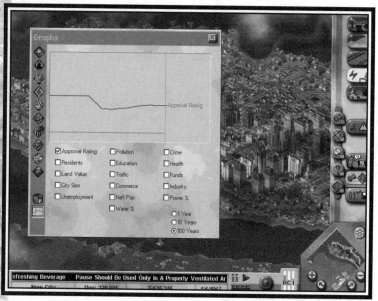

FIG. 13-2. YOUR APPROVAL RATING AS MAYOR CAN GO THROUGH UPS AND DOWNS (AND UPS ...).

Chapter 14
Finance

Here's where the rubber really meets the road. It's time to look at your city's financial world. *SimCity* finances, while considerably less complex than what happens out here in the "real" world, still present you with some challenges. In this chapter, we'll tour the various options available to you.

The Budget Window

You can access the Budget window at any time by clicking the Budget button in the control panel. This window is also displayed automatically at the first day of the new year, unless you have the Auto Budget option selected.

The Budget window has two parts, Expenditures and Income, which you can toggle between by clicking on the corresponding tab buttons at the top of the view. Below these are the current year and month, a list of the various line items in your budget, controls to let you adjust levels, and the year-to-date and year-end estimated expenses or income. From here, you can also meet with your various departmental advisors, as well as your overall budget advisor.

Expenditures

The Expenditures button in the Budget window shows you what's being spent to support your city and all the services it provides. From here, you can also go to the Ordinances, Neighbor Deals, and Loans windows where, if you make adjustments, the results are automatically reflected in the expenditure's year-to-date and year-end estimated expense figures. You can adjust the budgets for the individual departments—Education, Fire Department, Police, and so on—by moving the slider bars for each, placing the slider below, on, or above the marker line indicating 100 percent funding.

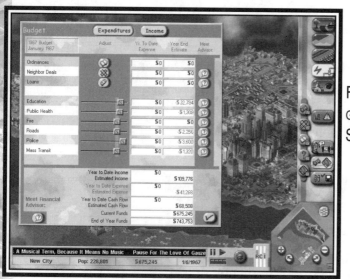

FIG. 14-1. THIS IS WHERE YOU GET TO DECIDE WHERE EVERY SIMOLEON GOES.

When you make adjustments to budget expenditures, such as enacting or repealing ordinances or moving the slider buttons, the figures in the expense columns will change. These columns report the year-to-date and year-end estimated costs for each line item, with totals at the bottom of the window.

It's important to note that the "Year-End Estimate" is exactly that. It represents the cost to your city budget, *assuming nothing else changes*. For example, if you later plop down several police stations in response to a crime wave, the actual expense could end up being much higher than the estimated figure. Conversely, if your police force gets fed up with being underpaid and having to drive police cars that haven't had an oil change since the beginning of the decade because of budget cuts—well, they may go on strike. However, you will continue to pay them at their previous rate of pay, so you get the worst of both worlds—reduced crime fighting and an ongoing budget drain. Furthermore, with the likely rise in crime, your SimCitizens will start moving away, eroding your tax base, further reducing available funds… And let us not forget, those striking police officers will be out there picketing, demanding a pay raise.

Hey, whoever said it was *easy* to be Mayor?

Ordinances

In the Expenditures portion of the Budget window, the Ordinances line item displays the cost of all enacted ordinances that require money to operate. For example, the Crossing Guard Ordinance hires Sims to stand on the more heavily trafficked city corners, helping poor pedestrian Sims to cross streets. Not only does this increase traffic slightly, but you also have to pay those crossing guards; so, it's an expense. Other ordinances actually produce income, but this information is broken out separately on the Income part of the Budget window.

The Ordinances adjust button takes you to the Ordinances window, where you can select and deselect city ordinances to your heart's content. As you select or deselect ordinances, the change in budget expenses to support them is reflected in the Budget window line item and totals.

FIG. 14-2. HERE'S WHERE YOU CAN SELECT AND DESELECT CITY ORDINANCES.

Neighbor Deals

The Neighbor Deals line item reflects actual and estimated spending on those deals costing you money. As with the Ordinances line item, those Neighbor Deals that add to your city's coffers are depicted in the Income portion of the Budget window.

Neighbor Deals costing money include:

- Purchasing water from a neighbor city
- Purchasing power from a neighbor city
- Exporting garbage to a neighbor city

FIG. 14-3. NEIGHBOR DEALS ARE ONE WAY OF DEALING WITH SHORTFALLS IN POWER, WATER, OR WASTE DISPOSAL CAPACITY.

Here, the year-end estimated cost can be even fuzzier than for other line items, because the estimate is calculated by multiplying the current month's usage times the number of months remaining in the year. At least with the departments, for example, you already know that if you build more roads, it's going to result in a higher budgetary outlay for maintaining them. For Neighbor Deals though, the effective usage rate can change on a monthly basis.

How's this, you may be asking? Let's say you've entered into a deal with Shelbyville to buy water for your parched (and water-pump deficient) city. You zone several new areas for construction. Sims start moving in, building houses and apartment buildings. Stores and strip malls go up. Cement plants and manufacturing facilities are built. All of these require water, and soon the sucking sound you hear atop the gurgling of water mains could be the sound of your cash flowing out to Shelbyville to pay for the needed water.

So, it's especially important to make sure that both your city infrastructure and your budget can handle unexpected variations in the use of Neighbor Deals.

Loans

As with Ordinances and Neighbor Deals, the Loans button takes you to the Loans window, where you can take out bonds to help keep your city afloat. The year-to-date column reflects the actual cost incurred on bonds outstanding, with the year-end estimate showing how much more will be paid through the end of the year on those bonds.

How loans work:

Loans come in §5,000 increments, up to §25,000 per loan.

You can elect to get a loan at any time, with no particular criteria or credit rating to satisfy.

A total of §250,000 is available for you to draw upon.

The interest rate is fixed at approximately 5 percent over the life of the loan. Payback is amortized over 10 years, with payment taken out of your city budget on a yearly basis.

There is no option to pay back early.

You can take out a maximum of 10 loans at any one time.

Loans are *not* factored into the evaluation for terminating a Mayor (that is, being §100,000 in the red), although that year's payment is counted.

Again, remember, if you take out new loans, this expense will go up, because payments begin immediately.

Departmental Budgets

Within the departmental budget area are a number of sub-categories that represent each of the city departments reporting to your mayoral office. These include:

- Police
- Fire
- Public Health
- Education
- Mass Transit
- Roads

The slider in the Budget window lets you adjust funding levels from 0 to 120 percent, with 100 percent funding being equal to the total number of assets (for example, police stations) multiplied by their listed annual maintenance cost.

Income

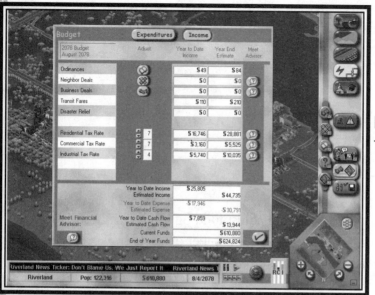

FIG. 14-5. HERE IS WHERE ALL THE MOOLAH COMES FROM.

Ordinances

In the Income portion of the Budget window, the City Ordinances line item displays the revenue generated by all enacted ordinances that produce money when operating. For example, the Industrial Pollutant Impact Fee not only encourages the conversion of dirty industry to clean industry, it also kicks in a small but decent revenue stream to your city's coffers.

Most other ordinances require funding, but this information is broken out separately on the Expenditures part of the Budget window.

For more details, see Chapter 15: Ordinances.

Neighbor Deals

This line item displays the sum of all income generated from Neighbor Deals, which could include:

- Selling water to a neighbor city
- Selling power to a neighbor city
- Importing a neighbor city's garbage

Note that this figure doesn't include the budgetary subtractions from Neighbor Deals that cost you money, which could include purchasing water or power from neighbors or exporting garbage. For that, you need to look at the Neighbor Deals line in the Expenditures part of the Budget window.

For more details, see Chapter 16: Neighbors.

Business Deals

This line shows the money generated by any active Business Deals you may have—that is, buildings you've constructed in your city. The revenue represents your payoff for putting up with the pollution, crime, and other nasty side effects of these buildings. They can include:

- Toxic Waste Factory
- Maximum Security Prison
- MegaMall
- Casino

FIG. 14-6. BUSINESS DEALS ARE ANOTHER WAY OF PADDING YOUR CITY'S COFFERS.

For more details, see the Chapter 17: Business Deals.

Transit Fares

Transit Fares are the income generated by ridership on your city's bus, rail, and subway systems (assuming you have them). This modest source of revenue has, in real life, often made the difference between a balanced budget and operating in the red. On the other hand, in the real world, there's only one subway system that survives without subsidies (Hong Kong's) and even that may no longer be true. Considering the expense of building and maintaining mass transit, fares are less a "source of revenue" than a way to partially recoup your costs.

There's one ordinance that can affect this line item: Subsidized Mass Transit. Available in 1940, this ordinance increases Sim ridership on mass transportation and increases the distance they're willing to travel. However, it cuts bus, rail, and subway fares by 50 percent, although the reduction in income is offset here by reductions in traffic congestion and air pollution.

Disaster Relief

Admit it: you've built up a nice big city, or maybe you've loaded one of the cities included with *SimCity 3000* and started hitting it with one disaster after another just to see what happens. It just goes to show you that kids aren't the only ones to build sand castles and then have a blast stomping them flat.

Well, in the event of disasters, whether you started them yourself or they just happened randomly, the Federal SimGovernment and the Sim Cross notice the news reports and take pity on your poor, suffering citizens. Aid is provided in the form of Disaster Relief, money dropped straight into your treasury to disburse as you see fit. Use it to put out the fires, bulldoze damaged areas, and rebuild—or you can use it to erect monuments to yourself and your enlightened rule. Your call.

The cost for a given disaster is calculated as follows:

(Cost of all civic buildings destroyed) + (cost to demolish all rubble tiles created by the disaster) + (cost of all network elements)

Disaster Relief is only awarded over a certain threshold, §500 Simoleons in total damage and repair costs. What you receive is 25 percent of the damage costs, with an additional 10 percent (for a total of 35 percent relief) if you managed to anticipate the disaster and issued the emergency warning in time.

RCI Tax Rates

SimCity 3000 uses an economy loosely based on the U.S. economy through the twentieth century and beyond (as predicted by the wizards at Maxis), showing varied demands for different products over time. Demand fluctuates and the economy shifts toward a service-oriented, commerce-based economy and from dirty industry to clean, high technology. You can use this to your advantage to build a better city.

You're given direct control over three kinds of tax "packages," each of which directly affects one of the three components of the city economy.

TABLE 14-1. TAX PACKAGES

RCI Slider	Types of Taxes Simulated
Residential	Personal income tax, residential property tax
Commercial	Sales tax, value added tax, commercial property tax
Industrial	Corporate income tax, industrial property tax

For more details about RCI, see the Chapter 6: Land Development and the RCI Model.

Strategies

Here are a few guidelines to help you in your quest for the perfectly balanced budget.

Incentives

One way to ride the waves of the economy successfully is to use taxes and incentives to your advantage. Low taxes will attract development; high taxes will drive it away.

The effects of taxation were dramatic in *SimCity Classic*, but played down somewhat in *SimCity 2000*. In *SimCity 3000*, understanding the use of tax rates is once again essential.

For example, although you can't affect RCI demand directly, you can have an immediate *indirect* effect on any one or all three zone demands by changing tax rates. Many of the ordinances also have effects on RCI demand—and not coincidentally, on your budgetary bottom line. The precise effects are described in more detail in Chapter 6: Land Development and the RCI Model.

In general, there's going to be too much demand for Residential property, so it can usually tolerate higher taxes. Plus, it gives you the most revenue per month, so having slightly higher taxes on Residential is a good plan. Lowering taxes on Industry is a good way to spur Industrial growth and boost demand for Residential if you get in a rut.

Overfunding/Underfunding

You have the option to overfund or underfund each of the departmental budgets, adjustable via sliders in the Budget Expenditures window.

Overfunding

Overfunding, or spending more than 100 percent of the required budget for a department, has the following effects:

- Police and Fire: eliminates any danger of a strike
- Schools and Hospitals: slightly increases the number of EQ/HQ points provided by each service, eliminates the danger of a strike
- Mass Transit: eliminates strike danger
- Road Maintenance: repairs potholes and infrastructure and eliminates danger of a strike

For the top three, overfunding will have some positive effect to department effectiveness, but it is a case of diminishing returns.

Overfunding above 110 percent can also result in news ticker announcements about how happy your workers are with your budgetary decisions. Although it's nice to be loved, that's not what they're paying you for now, is it?

Underfunding

Underfunding, or spending less than 100 percent of the required budget for a department, has the following effects:

- Police and Fire: reduces the radius of influence for stations while maintaining effectiveness within that radius; increases the likelihood of strike proportionally to the degree of underfunding
- Schools and Hospitals: reduces the number of EQ/HQ points provided by each service, increases the likelihood of strike proportionally to the degree of underfunding
- Mass Transit: increases the likelihood of a strike proportionally to the degree of underfunding
- Road Maintenance: roads develop potholes, meaning Sims will be slowed on their trips to destinations, possibly causing trips to fail altogether

Finances in General

- As funding decreases, the efficiency of each department decreases linearly, creating noticeable effects at funding levels even just a little less than 100 percent. For example, as funding is cut, the radius of effectiveness for police stations and Fire Department shrinks quickly toward zero.
- As funding increases, the efficiency of each department increases hyperbolically, creating noticeable effects at funding levels even just a little higher than 100 percent, but with rapidly diminishing returns. For example, as funding is increased, the boost in EQ/HQ for schools and hospitals begins tailing off after the first 5 or 10 percent of overfunding.

Deficit Spending and Operating in the Red

If deficit spending is good enough for national, state, and local governments across the globe, it's good enough for you, right?

Well, it's never quite so simple. Spending money you don't have can drive a thriving, vibrant city straight into the ground. Moreover, having no available money means you can't buy anything either. You can't zone new areas, build needed facilities, or expand. On top of all this, if the deficit gets too high, you've got big problems—§100,000 Simoleons of red ink will get you fired from your position as Mayor.

Still, sometimes you may have no choice. Or you might have decided to keep your tax rate super low to encourage growth and are waiting out a recession. In any case, it's usually best if you can stay in the black.

Auto Budget

Setting the Auto Budget toggle to "on" has several effects:

- The year-end budget summary isn't displayed unless you are projected to lose money in that year.
- Unless you changed them manually beforehand, RCI tax rates are all set to 7 percent and funding (for any active department) is set to 100 percent for all departments.
- For departments that are activated while Auto Budget is on—for example, if you drop your first police station, Fire Department, or school—the budget for the department is automatically set to 100 percent.

Chapter 15
City Ordinances

It's good to be Mayor.

True, the "little people," the Sims, will come to you from time to time, petitioning for this or that. Ultimately though, the decision is yours. By placing zones, roads, and services, you design the overall plan for your city. Ordinances are a way of "tweaking" the day-to-day and year-to-year operation, possibly solving or alleviating minor problems or even steering the overall direction in which your city will develop. They also help in subtle but far-reaching ways in determining whether your city will grow or decline.

City ordinances fall into seven broad categories:

- Utilities: affect the availability and consumption of power and water
- Health, Education, and Aura (HEA): improve the overall quality of life for your Sims, helping them live longer, learn more, and lead happier lives
- Public Safety: reduce crime, fire risks, traffic, and accidents
- Environment: help control garbage and keep pollution in check
- City Planning: reduce damage in the event of disasters, encourage growth, and improve land values
- Transportation: enable your Sims to travel further, more efficiently, and reduce overall traffic
- Finance: bring in funds above and beyond taxes

Some ordinances are available to you at the start of the game, others become available as time goes by or when certain events occur. Each ordinance has pros and cons, and costs or revenues.

Accessing Ordinances

You can access the ordinance window through several places. One is the Budget window, by selecting the "Adjust" button on either the Expenditures or Income windows. You can also select the Ordinances button on the right toolbar.

FIG. 15-1. YOU CAN ACCESS THE ORDINANCE WINDOW THROUGH THE EXPENDITURE WINDOW ...

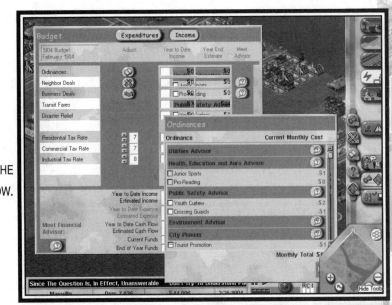

FIG. 15-2. ... OR THROUGH THE INCOME WINDOW.

You can also get to the ordinances by selecting the "Review Ordinances" button in the advisors' dialogs.

FIG. 15-3. YOUR TRUSTED ADVISORS ARE READY AND ABLE TO DISCUSS AT ANY TIME THE ORDINANCES AVAILABLE TO YOU.

Ordinances are grouped by the area they most affect, although it's important to note that many can have an impact on other factors. For example, the Parking Fine Ordinance can add a nice little boost to your monthly income and lowers traffic, but it sure can make the Sims who get the tickets quite irate.

Each ordinance category has an "Ask Advisor" button that brings you to the appropriate Advisors' Briefings window. This window will display descriptions of each currently available ordinance in that advisor's area. Your can also access the window through the right toolbar.

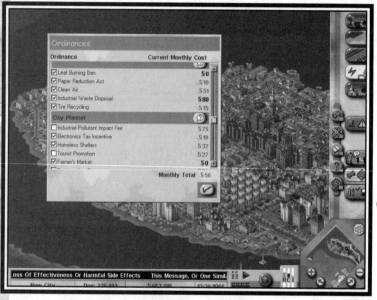

FIG. 15-4. ORDINANCES ARE POWERFUL TOOLS TO SUBTLY BUT EFFECTIVELY STEER THE DIRECTION OF YOUR CITY'S GROWTH.

To activate an ordinance, check the box to the left of the ordinance. Like all expenses and revenues, the financial effect of the ordinance is calculated based on monthly rates and the remainder of the year, with adjustments made to the city budget at the end of the year.

To help in your decision whether to enact, repeal, or ignore a given ordinance, the financial impact of each ordinance is displayed. Active ordinances have their financial impact displayed in solid color, inactive ordinances have the value grayed out.

New Ordinances

New ordinances, those which become available after the beginning of the game, are triggered by Petitioners. When a new ordinance becomes available, four things happen:

- A news ticker announcement informs you that a Petitioner wishes to speak with you on this matter
- Your advisor in that area will list the new ordinance in the Advisor Briefings window, and from there you can get more details
- The Meet Petitioner window lists the request
- The ordinance is added to the Ordinance window, but left inactive

You can activate the new ordinance either by going to the Ordinance window and checking the activation box or by choosing the "yes" response to the Petitioner's request.

FIG. 15-5. YOU CAN APPROVE NEW ORDINANCES THROUGH THE ORDINANCE WINDOW OR BY AGREEING IMMEDIATELY TO THE PETITIONER'S REQUEST.

Ordinance Summary

The following tables list all of the ordinances, along with a basic summary of their availability and effects.

TABLE 15-1. UTILITIES ORDINANCE SUMMARY

Name	Year Available	Notes
Stairwell Lighting	1930	—
Mandatory Water Meters	1930	—
Water Conservation	1960	—
Power Conservation	1970	—

TABLE 15-2. HEALTH, EDUCATION, AND AURA (HEA) ORDINANCE SUMMARY

Name	Year Available	Notes
Junior Sports	Always	Not petitioned until you have a school
Pro-Reading Campaign	Always	Not petitioned until you have a Library
Free Clinics	1960	—
Nuclear Free Zone	1990	—
Public Smoking Ban	1990	—
Community CPR Training	1970	—

Monthly Cost	Effects Pro	Effects Con
§0.0001/Sim	Decreases power consumption	Costs money
§0.0006/Sim	Lowers water consumption	Costs money
§0.00024/Sim	Lowers water consumption	Costs money and lowers demand for Industrial
§0.0004/building area	Lowers building power consumption for Industrial	Costs money and lowers demand

Monthly Cost	Effects Pro	Effects Con
§0.00007/Sim	Decreases crime and increases EQ	Costs money
§0.0000125/Sim plus the number of libraries	Increases EQ	Costs money
§0.0001/Sim	Increases LE	Costs money
§0.00003/Sim	Increases Aura	Can't place Nuclear power plants; if any exist when ordinance is enacted, they disappear (but don't explode)
§0.0006/Sim	Increases LE	Costs money
§0.00003/Sim	Increases LE	Costs money

Name	Year Available	Notes

Table 15-3. Public Safety Ordinance Summary

Name	Year Available	Notes
Crossing Guards	Always	Not petitioned until more than 250 road tiles exist
Youth Curfew	Always	Not available until Police Station exists
Neighborhood Watch	1970	—
Mandatory Smoke Detectors	1970	—

Name	Year Available	Notes

Table 15-4. Environmental Ordinance Summary

Name	Year Available	Notes
Industrial Waste Disposal Tax	1950	Not petitioned until Commercial plus Industrial tiles are greater than 3,000
Tire Recycling	1940	—
Clean Air	1950	—
Leaf Burning Ban	1960	—
Paper Reduction Act	1960	—
Backyard Composting	1970	—
Lawn Chemical Ban	1970	—
Mandatory Car Smogging	1980	—
Trash Presort	1980	—
Landfill Gas Recovery	1990	—

Monthly Cost	Effects Pro	Effects Con
§0.0005/Sim	Increases LE	Costs money and increases global traffic by 3 percent
§0.0001/Sim plus the number of Police Stations	Lowers global crime and raises youth EQ	Costs money
§0.000056/Sim	Lowers global crime	Costs money
§0.001/building area	Lowers global flammability	Costs money

Monthly Cost	Effects Pro	Effects Con
Raises §0.00005/Sim	Decreases garbage and raises money	Lowers demand for Commercial and Industrial
§0.000025/Sim	Decreases garbage, decreases maintenance cost for new road and highway tiles	Costs money
§0.0002/Sim	Lowers air pollution, demand for dirty industry	Costs money
None	Lowers air pollution and flammability	Increases garbage
§0.00002/Sim	Lowers garbage	Costs money
§0.00002/Sim	Lowers garbage	Costs money
§0.00006/Sim	Lowers water pollution	Costs money and slows farmland development
§0.00008/Sim	Decreases air pollution	Costs money and lowers Aura
§0.00007/Sim plus number of recycling centers	Lowers global garbage by 10 percent	Costs money
§0.000035/Sim	Lowers air pollution	Costs money

TABLE 15-5. CITY PLANNER ORDINANCE SUMMARY

Name	Year Available	Notes
Farmers' Market	Always	Petitioner should show up early in the game
Earthquake Resistance and Retrofitting	Always	Number of all developed tiles must be greater than 1,000
Homeless Shelters	Always	Unemployment must be greater than 4 percent
Tourist Promotion	Always	Developed Commercial tiles must be greater than 200
Industrial Pollutant Impact Fee	1950	Developed Industrial tiles must be greater than 500
Conservation Corps	1915	—
Clean Industry Association	1930	—
Electronics Tax Incentive	1950	—
Aerospace Tax Incentive	1960	Must have airport
Electronics Job Fair	1970	—
Biotech Tax Incentive	1980	—
Public Access Cable	1980	This is intentionally a money sucker

TABLE 15-6. TRANSPORTATION ORDINANCE SUMMARY

Name	Year Available	Notes
Parking Fines	Always	A good way to get extra money early on
Shuttle Service	Always	Must have bus, rail, or subway in your city
Subsidized Mass Transit	1940	Must have bus, rail, or subway in your city
Alternate Day Driving	1950	—
Carpool Incentive	1980	—

TABLE 15-7. FINANCIAL ORDINANCE SUMMARY

Name	Year Available	Notes
Legalized Gambling	Always	Petitioned after population is greater than 1,000

Monthly Cost	Effects Pro	Effects Con
No cost	Increases farm development	None, unless you don't like farms
§0.001/building area	Minimizes earthquake damage	Costs money
§0.00014/Sim	Increases global land value	Costs moneyTourist Promotion
§0.00028/Sim	Increases Commercial demand	Costs money and increases global traffic
Raises §0.000023/Sim	Lowers dirty industry demand and decreases pollution, raises money	Lowers Industrial demand
§0.00033/Sim	Decreases crime, water pollution, and garbage	Costs money and lowers Industrial demand
§0.00039/Sim	Increases clean industry demand, decreases dirty industry demand	Costs money
§0.0003/Sim	Increases clean industry demand	Costs money
§0.0003/Sim	Increases clean industry demand	Costs money
§0.0003/Sim	Increases clean industry demand	Costs money
§0.0003/Sim	Increases clean industry demand	Costs money
§0.0003/Sim	Increases clean industry demand	Costs money

Monthly Cost	Effects Pro	Effects Con
Raises §0.00065/Sim	Raises money and decreases global traffic	Lowers aura
§0.0008/Sim	Sims travel one tile farther than normal before giving up	Costs money
Cuts mass transit revenues in half	Increases Sim ridership on mass transit	Costs money
§0.0001/Sim	Decreases global traffic	Costs money and lowers Aura
§0.00065/Sim	Decreases global traffic	Costs money

Monthly Cost	Effects Pro	Effects Con
Raises §0.001/Sim	Brings in money and allows for Casino	Increases crime

Detailed Ordinance Descriptions

The following section gives specific details on the general categories for ordinances, when the individual ordinances become available, their fiscal impact, pros, cons, and general comments on each.

Utilities

Stairwell Lighting

Year available: 1930
Monthly fiscal impact: Minus §0.0001 per Sim
Pro: Increases power plant capacity (by decreasing consumption)
Con: Costs money
Notes: Stairwell lighting is for tall Commercial buildings mainly
Comments: Requires all high-occupancy buildings to install small automatic devices called "minuterie" in public stairwells. These devices detect movement and turn off lights when the stairwell is not in use, saving energy. This ordinance has a small monthly cost based on number of buildings, but it benefits the city by reducing overall power consumption.

Mandatory Water Meters

Year available: 1930
Monthly fiscal impact: Minus §0.0006 per Sim
Pro: Reduces water demand
Con: Costs money
Comments: Requires water meters to be placed in all buildings within the city limits. Building owners are assessed water usage fees based on actual water consumption for that building. Up to half of this assessment may be passed on to building tenants and renters. The city incurs a monthly cost to support this ordinance, an amount based on the number of buildings in the city. Funds are used to pay for meter installation and periodic meter readings. Its effects are to significantly reduce citywide water consumption.

Water Conservation

Year available: 1960
Monthly fiscal impact: Minus §0.00024 per Sim
Pro: Lowers water consumption
Con: Costs money and reduces demand for industry
Comments: Funds citywide programs to educate Sims about methods to reduce residential water consumption. In addition, it sets restrictive standards for business water usage, sending in undercover spies to procure evidence against any business that is not in full compliance. The monthly cost for maintaining this ordinance is based on city population. When enacted, water consumption in the city drops by several percentage points.

Power Conservation

Year available: 1970
Monthly fiscal impact: Minus §0.0004 per Sim and total building area
Pro: Reduces power consumption
Con: Costs money, lowers demand for industry
Comments: Funds programs to teach Sims about methods for reducing power consumption at home, including turning off air conditioners and cable TV sets. Residents are asked for voluntary compliance, but businesses must adhere to mandatory power restrictions and receive large fines for noncompliance. When enacted, power consumption in the city drops by several percentage points.

Health, Education, and Aura

Junior Sports

Year available: Always
Monthly fiscal impact: Minus §0.00007 per Sim
Pro: Reduces crime and boosts EQ

Con: Costs money

Notes: Petitioner not triggered until you have built at least one school

Comments: The Junior Sports Ordinance organizes after-school team sports for youths. Uniforms are provided by various companies in the city in a spirit of cooperation with local government. Still, the ordinance costs the city a small amount each month based on city population. Crime in the city is lowered by giving young troublemakers a positive outlet for impertinent creativity. And all students in the league show a marked increase in standardized test scores thanks to strict academic requirements.

Pro-Reading Campaign

Year available: Always

Monthly fiscal impact: Minus §0.0000125 per Sim plus §1 per Library

Pro: Boosts EQ

Con: Costs money

Notes: Petitioner not triggered until you have built at least one Library

Comments: Promotes reading and writing in the city through the use of tutors, special programs, and other learning resources. All Sims especially younger ones, may take advantage of these free extracurricular classes to improve reading skills, learn new skills, or just get out of the house on occasion. This ordinance has a monthly cost based on city population. It brings positive effects to the Sims, including an overall increase in the city's education levels.

Free Clinics

Year available: 1960

Monthly fiscal impact: Minus §0.0001 per Sim

Pro: Boosts LE

Con: Costs money

Comments: The Free Clinics Ordinance uses city funds to establish and maintain low-cost, high-efficiency clinics. Although they are open to the entire citizenry, these clinics are generally frequented by members of the lower economic strata, and thus treat a wide variety of ailments which would otherwise go untreated. The monthly cost of this ordinance is based on population. It results in a general rise in the city's health, and the sense of having done something worthwhile.

Nuclear Free Zone

Year available: 1990
Monthly fiscal impact: Minus §0.00003 per Sim
Pro: Increases Aura
Con: Cannot place Nuclear power plants or missile silos; if your city has these things, they're removed instantly. Also costs money, although not very much.
Comments: The Nuclear Free Zone Ordinance spends a small amount of money per Sim on promotion of alternatives to nuclear applications and the replacement of existing nuclear facilities. Politically charged and occasionally effectual, this ordinance raises a city's Aura by providing Sims with a feeling of impact in an otherwise uncaring world. Note, however, that if any nukes are removed by enacting this ordinance, it's by dismantling them, not explosion.

Public Smoking Ban

Year available: 1990
Monthly fiscal impact: Minus §0.0006 per Sim
Pro: Boosts LE
Con: Costs money
Comments: The Public Smoking Ban outlaws smoking in and around all public buildings. The city must pay money each month, an amount based on population, to equip local merchants with plastic water buckets. When this ordinance is in effect, the result is an increase in the overall health of city Sims.

Community CPR Training

Year available: 1970
Monthly fiscal impact: Minus §0.0003 per Sim
Pro: Raises LE
Con: Costs money
Comments: The Community CPR Training Ordinance spends city funds each month (an amount based on population) to establish medical training centers around the city. Sims are encouraged to learn, free of charge, emergency life-saving techniques that can increase survival rates for Sims who experience cardiac arrest. Conducted by local chapters of the Junior Llama League, this program raises general health levels of the populace and gives all Sims peace of mind.

Public Safety

Crossing Guards

Year available: Always
Monthly fiscal impact: Minus §0.0005 per Sim
Pro: Increases overall LE
Con: Increases global traffic by three percent, and of course, costs money
Notes: Not petitioned until more than 250 road tiles exist in your city
Comments: Puts highly trained crossing guards at some of the more challenging intersections of the city. This ordinance carries a small monthly cost, based on population, to pay the salaries of these fearless public servants. Crossing guards help prevent pedestrian accidents, increasing the overall health of Sims in the city. However, traffic becomes more congested at these intersections, causing a slight increase in citywide traffic.

Youth Curfew

Year available: Always
Monthly fiscal impact: Minus §0.0001 per Sim and the number of Police Stations

Pro: Lowers crime, boosts youth EQ

Con: Costs money

Notes: Available only after at least one police station has been built. After all, you can't have a police patrol to pick up young delinquents if you don't have a station.

Comments: The Youth Curfew reduces crime by requiring that all Sims under age 22 be off the streets by 10:00 p.m. every night. Violators are escorted to the nearest police station, where they must wait for their parents or guardians to take them home. This ordinance has a monthly cost, based on city population. Funds are used to pay for the additional police patrols needed.

Mandatory Smoke Detectors

Year available: 1970

Monthly fiscal impact: Minus §0.001 per building

Pro: Lowers flammability

Con: Costs money

Comments: Requires that smoke detectors be installed in all buildings, public or private. These battery-powered devices emit a piercing sound whenever smoke is present. As irritating as the noise is, Sims prefer this harmless annoyance to the alternative—being unaware a fire has broken out. When enacted, citywide flammability is significantly lowered.

Neighborhood Watch

Year available: 1970

Monthly fiscal impact: Minus §0.00005 per Sim

Pro: Lowers crime globally

Con: Costs money

Comments: Allocates a small amount of money per Sim each month to promote and maintain a police rapid-response program with member neighborhoods. Funds are used to pay for signs announcing the program, and to equip each block captain with equipment. This program helps lower overall crime in the city.

Environment

Industrial Waste Disposal Tax

Year available: 1950
Monthly fiscal impact: Plus §0.00005 per Sim
Pro: Generates money and reduces garbage produced and brings in money
Con: Lowers demand for Commercial and Industrial
Notes: Available after number of Commercial and Industrial tiles is greater than 3,000
Comments: A tax on all Commercial and Industrial interests doing business in the city to pay for special disposal of Class 3 refuse. To "share the burden," a flat tax is assessed to all businesses regardless of the actual amount of Class 3 refuse they produce. All companies dislike this tax, particularly small business owners who feel the flat tax structure is unfair. This ordinance brings monthly revenue into the treasury, an amount based on the number of Commercial and Industrial buildings in the city. It tends to lower Commercial and Industrial demand.

Tire Recycling

Year available: 1940
Monthly fiscal impact: Minus §0.000025 per Sim
Pro: Reduces garbage produced; also reduces maintenance cost of new road tiles
Con: Costs money
Comments: Requires that all discarded vehicular tires be pulverized and incorporated into asphalt, in accordance with common road engineering practices. This ordinance reduces both garbage production and the cost of building new roads. A monthly fee, based on Sim population, is deducted from the treasury when this ordinance is in effect. Funds pay for pulverizing the city's old tires, and delivering the material to the Transportation Department for use in road construction.

Clean Air

Year available: 1950
Monthly fiscal impact: Minus §0.0002 per Sim
Pro: Lowers pollution, discourages dirty industry
Con: Costs money, also discourages dirty industry
Comments: Looks for ways to demonstrate and promote reduced air pollution techniques, especially to industry. The overall effect is to lower citywide air pollution. Industry may see itself as the victim of this measure, especially when forced to clean up its own mess.

Leaf Burning Ban

Year available: 1960
Monthly fiscal impact: None
Pro: Lowers air pollution and flammability
Con: Increases garbage
Comments: Asks residents to refrain from setting outdoor fires to dispose of piles of leaves. Sims are still free to burn their leaves in their living rooms, should they choose to do so. The result is a reduction of citywide air pollution and a lowering of flammability. Unless and until the City Council approves the distribution of free plastic lawn and leaf bags, there's no monthly cost associated with this ordinance.

Paper Reduction Act

Year available: 1960
Monthly fiscal impact: Minus §0.00002 per Sim
Pro: Reduces garbage produced
Con: Costs money
Comments: Reduces garbage levels in the city by calling attention to the vast amount of paper wasted in the normal course of running a business. It requires all production managers to file a 50-page report whenever paper usage at their business or factory exceeds, by 10 percent or more, the previous month's levels. These reports

are to be typed on the Standard Form 23/6-A (rev. 2), and must provide written justification for the paper usage variance. The monthly cost of this ordinance, based on Sim population, pays to bind and store these reports in public reading rooms. The ordinance is found to be an effective means for reducing garbage production, because managers will do "whatever it takes" to avoid writing a report.

Backyard Composting

Year available: 1970
Monthly fiscal impact: Minus §0.00002 per Sim
Pro: Reduces garbage produced
Con: Costs money
Comments: Establishes periodic neighborhood workshops to train citizens in the techniques of composting, a process that converts organic home refuse into a useful fertilizer. The monthly cost of this ordinance, based on Sim population, helps cover the budget for workshops. It benefits the city by reducing citywide garbage and by letting Sims experience the good feeling that comes when one works the soil.

Lawn Chemical Ban

Year available: 1970
Monthly fiscal impact: Minus §0.00006 per Sim
Pro: Reduces water pollution
Con: Costs money, slows farmland development
Comments: Forbids the use of any fertilizer that contains Triphenel-Bichloral-Monodioxide, a compound that has been found to contaminate the city's ground water. Although the chemical ban hinders agricultural development, most Sims believe the reduction in water pollution is for the greater good. Each month the city is charged a fee (based on population) to pay for research and development of safer fertilizers, a move to appease farmers and persnickety gardeners who rely on the 3P-2B-1D compound to control weeds.

Mandatory Car Smogging

Year available: 1980
Monthly fiscal impact: Minus §0.00008 per Sim
Pro: Reduces air pollution
Con: Costs money and decreases Aura
Comments: Requires that any car driven comply in principle with clean emissions standards as set by the International Geo-Physical Council of 1979. When this ordinance is enacted, air pollution levels drop. The city spends money each month for administration of the program, an amount which varies based on population. And since the cost of noncompliance falls upon the car owners, a few Sims are always very annoyed by this ordinance.

Trash Presort

Year available: 1980
Monthly fiscal impact: Minus §0.00007 per Sim plus §1 per Recycling Center
Pro: Decreases global garbage by 10 percent
Con: Costs money
Comments: The Trash Presort Ordinance encourages Sims to separate their garbage for more efficient recycling. Individual bins are provided for each refuse type.

Landfill Gas Recovery

Year available: 1990
Monthly fiscal impact: Minus §0.000035 per Sim
Pro: Reduces air pollution
Con: Costs money
Comments: The Landfill Gas Recovery Project instructs the city to use available technology to recover that natural gas that is a by-product of garbage decomposition in a landfill. The city may, at its discretion, build and maintain its own recovery plants, contract such recovery to local businesses, or both. Any recovered natural gas will revert to the Utilities Department for inclusion in the city's general power production,

although the amounts are not expected to be significant. When this ordinance is in effect, the city incurs a small monthly cost that fluctuates with population. However, air pollution will be reduced by this project, making the whole thing worthwhile.

City Planning

Farmers' Market

Year available: Always
Monthly fiscal impact: None (they're free!)
Pro: Increases farm development
Con: None
Comments: The Farmers' Market Ordinance, the brainchild of the Urban and Rural Resource Sharing Committee, asks the city to allocate a parcel of land where farmers can sell fresh fruits and vegetables to the public at wholesale prices. There are no costs to the city for enacting this ordinance, and all its effects are positive. It encourages farm development in nearby areas, and gives Sims a place to go on Saturday mornings.

Earthquake Resistance and Retrofitting

Year available: Always
Monthly fiscal impact: Minus §0.001 per building area
Pro: Minimizes damage in the event of an earthquake
Con: Costs money
Notes: Number of all developed tiles must be greater than 1,000
Comments: This ordinance requires that money be spent on design, engineering and construction of earthquake-resistant buildings, and also on retrofitting older buildings constructed before the advent of modern techniques. When the Earthquake Resistance and Retrofitting Ordinance is enacted, buildings sustain less severe damage during an earthquake than they ordinarily would incur. It can be pricey though, since the amount of money spent monthly to support this ordinance is based on the number and types of buildings in the city.

Homeless Shelters

Year available: Always
Monthly fiscal impact: Minus §0.00014 per Sim
Pro: Boosts global land value
Con: Costs money
Notes: Unemployment must be greater than four percent
Comments: Pays for shelters, soup lines, and basic infrastructure to aid the city's less fortunate. The ordinance incurs a monthly cost based on city population. The money seems well spent, as the city's overall land value actually increases.

Tourist Promotion

Year available: Always
Monthly fiscal impact: Minus §0.00028 per Sim
Pro: Increases Commercial demand
Con: Costs money, increases traffic
Notes: Developed Commercial tiles must be greater than 200 for this ordinance to be available
Comments: Uses tried-and-true advertising techniques to attract tourists to town. More tourists mean more Commercial demand, so this ordinance spurs city growth by attracting nonpolluting businesses to the city. Each month, advertising costs are deducted from the city treasury in an amount based on the number of existing Commercial buildings. Sims benefit from a stronger Commercial demand, and cleaner air. On the other hand, they are less enamored with the traffic that the shutter-happy tourists bring.

Industrial Pollutant Impact Fee

Year available: 1950
Monthly fiscal impact: Plus §0.000023 per Sim
Pro: Decreases dirty industry demand, decreases pollution, raises money
Con: Decreases industrial demand
Notes: Developed Industrial tiles must be greater than 500 for this ordinance to be available
Comments: Assesses a monthly fee to each polluting factory in the city. Fees are deposited into the city treasury with the understanding that someday they may be needed to clean up dangerously contaminated sites. Industry seems to resent government regulation in any form, and some factories may respond by moving to less restrictive cities. As long as the ordinance is in place, it may be difficult to persuade new industries to move in, replacing those that leave.

Conservation Corps

Year available: 1915
Monthly fiscal impact: Minus §0.00033 per Sim
Pro: Increases clean industry demand, decreases crime, decreases water pollution, decreases garbage
Con: Costs money
Comments: An organization responsible for maintaining the natural beauty of the city. Armed with litter-stabbing sticks and plastic trash bags, Sims of the Corps can be seen patrolling city highways, streets, and coastlines hunting down unsightly trash. This ordinance is funded through a monthly fee based on the number of polluting factories in the city. In addition to reducing pollution and helping to attract clean industry, the Conservation Corps keeps teenagers busy with positive activities and a sense of purpose, helping to reduce crime.

Clean Industry Association

Year available: 1930
Monthly fiscal impact: Minus §0.00039 per Sim
Pro: Increases clean industry demand, decreases dirty industry demand, decreases pollution
Con: Costs money
Comments: The Clean Industry Association is a consortium of cities that promote clean industry throughout SimNation. A small monthly fee supports the association's efforts to attract nonpolluting industries, conduct research in waste management, and act as a watchdog over polluting Industrial sites. Many a new mayor has welcomed high-polluting industries into the city, only to regret the eventual costs to the quality of life. Enacting this ordinance will please ecologically-minded residents, but when polluting industries start feeling the pressure, they may pack up their dirty bags and leave—which may be just what you're after.

Electronics Tax Incentive

Year available: 1950
Monthly fiscal impact: Minus §0.0003 per Sim
Pro: Increases clean industry demand
Con: Costs money
Comments: Designed to attract electronics companies to your city by subsidizing some of the taxes those companies would otherwise pay. Even for cities only mildly attractive to the electronics industry, this tax break can give companies a reason to take a second look. The monthly cost of this subsidy can be pricey. But if moving toward cleaner industry is on your agenda, the financial hit may be worth it.

Aerospace Tax Incentive

Year available: 1960
Monthly fiscal impact: Minus §0.0003 per Sim
Pro: Increases clean industry demand
Con: Costs money
Notes: You must also have an Airport built to get this ordinance
Comments: Attracts developers of aerospace materials to your city by subsidizing some of the tax burden those companies would otherwise pay. This may encourage Industrial demand in your city, depending on the growth of the aerospace industry.

Electronics Job Fair

Year available: 1970
Monthly fiscal impact: Minus §0.0003 per Sim
Pro: Increases clean industry demand
Con: Costs money
Comments: Pays for an annual city-sponsored job fair. Electronics companies view the job fair as a valuable way to find an educated and experienced employee base, and are more likely to set up in cities that hold one. Demand for clean industry increases when this ordinance is enacted, but the city foots the bill, which is a monthly fee based on population.

Biotech Tax Incentive

Year available: 1980
Monthly fiscal impact: Minus §0.0003 per Sim
Pro: Increases clean industry demand
Con: Costs money
Comments: Attracts biotechnology companies to your city by subsidizing a portion of the taxes those companies would otherwise pay. This encourages industrial demand (depending on the growth of the biotechnology industry), but the aggregate cost of the subsidy, is deducted from the treasury each month.

Public Access Cable

Year available: 1980
Monthly fiscal impact: Minus §0.0003 per Sim
Pro: Increases clean industry demand
Con: Costs money
Comments: Pays for free local use of media facilities by members of your community. Media companies are more likely to see your city as a place where telecommunication skills are highly valued, and may be more likely to move in, hoping to find an experienced employee base.

Transportation

Parking Fines

Year available: Always
Monthly fiscal impact: Plus §0.0006 per Sim
Pro: Generates money, lowers traffic
Con: Decreases Aura
Comments: Gives the city a small but steady source of income from parking violators. Dedicated city employees, patrol the streets and issue tickets to Sims who stop their cars without regard to safety factors, posted regulations, common courtesy, or civic pride. Enacting this ordinance tends to improve traffic flow in the city, but receiving parking tickets fuels the fire of Sims with latent anger issues.

Shuttle Service

Year available: Always

Monthly fiscal impact: Minus §0.0008 per Sim

Pro: Sims travel one tile farther than normal before giving up trips

Con: Costs money

Notes: Must have bus, rail, or subway service in your city for this ordinance to be available

Comments: Sims will normally walk only a short distance from their homes or offices to reach a road or mass transit stop. Enacting the Shuttle Service Ordinance sets up free shuttles around the city, increasing the distance Sims can travel to find other sources of transportation. The monthly cost of this ordinance is based on city population. Money is spent on repair and maintenance of a fleet of shuttles.

Subsidized Mass Transit

Year available: 1940

Monthly fiscal impact: Amount for each trip is cut in half

Pro: Increases Sim ridership on mass transportation and increases the distance they're willing to travel

Con: Costs money

Notes: Bus, subway, or rail service must exist in your city for this ordinance to be available

Comments: Cuts subway, rail and bus fares by 50 percent, providing an incentive for Sims to forego their cars for mass transit alternatives. City funds provide the subsidy, and an amount based on population is calculated and deducted from the treasury each month. This ordinance reduces traffic congestion and air pollution in the city.

Alternate Day Driving

Year available: 1950
Monthly fiscal impact: Minus §0.0001 per Sim
Pro: Lowers traffic
Con: Costs money and decreases Aura
Comments: Funds educational programs to promote the advantages of alternate day driving. Sims with even numbered license plates are encouraged to drive only on even days and those with odd numbered plates only on odd days. Drivers with vanity plates are asked to stay off the roads completely. Administering the program has a slight cost each month, based on population. Voluntary compliance with the Alternate Day Driving Ordinance reduces global traffic in the city.

Carpool Incentive

Year available: 1980
Monthly fiscal impact: Minus §0.0006 per Sim
Pro: Lowers global traffic by five percent
Con: Costs money
Comments: Encourages drivers to have passengers in their cars. Drivers with three additional passengers aren't required to stop for toll plazas. This ordinance has a monthly cost based on population to pay for administration of the program. The main benefit of this incentive is that it reduces traffic in the city, although at times tempers can flare.

Finance

Legalized Gambling

Year available: Always

Monthly fiscal impact: Plus §0.001 per Sim

Pro: Generates money. Also permits the building of a Casino.

Con: Increases crime

Notes: Petitioned after population is over 1,000

Comments: Legalized Gambling allows the establishment of Casinos offering card, table, and mechanical games of chance. The city regulates and takes a percentage of profits from all city gambling establishments each month. Even though gambling boosts the treasury, it attracts unsavory types prone to petty crime.

Chapter 16
Neighbors

New to *SimCity 3000* is the feature of Neighbor Deals. These are business arrangements with your adjacent city neighbors for the purchase or sale of water, power, or garbage.

By selling your excess water, power, or landfill capacity, you add money to the city treasury. On the other hand, you not only have to manage the extra demands to your city's infrastructure, there's also the possibility of hefty penalties if you can't keep up your end of the contract.

By buying water, power, or garbage disposal, you can meet shortfalls of these necessary resources, reducing the need to build additional water pumps, power plants, or landfills. However, the cost can be significant, especially if you come to depend on these sources.

How you use Neighbor Deals is entirely up to you. Ignore them, if you like, and build a city that doesn't need nothin' from nobody, thank you very much. Wheel and deal, if you'd prefer, and you might even be able to go so far as to have a city with no water pumps, no power plants, and no unsightly landfills or incinerators at all!

You also can use Neighbor Deals on a short-term basis, selling excess resources until you need them yourself or buying resources to meet short-term needs. Or, you can aim toward a city "philosophy" of being a major regional resource provider, or of letting your neighbors carry the burden of meeting your needs and dealing with the excess pollution and garbage.

The decision, as always, is yours. (Doesn't that feel terrific?)

Neighbor Deal Rules

To see what Neighbor Deals you're currently involved in or to explore the possibility of starting a deal, select the Neighbor Map.

FIG. 16-1. NEIGHBOR DEALS ALLOW YOU TO BUY AND SELL WATER, POWER, AND GARBAGE HANDLING.

At the bottom of the display is a list of your current deals, including the neighbor's name, the type of deal, and the current rate and financial impact on your budget. To get a Neighbor Deal, however, a certain number of conditions must be met, and it behooves you to understand all the implications.

Connection:

For a deal of any kind to be struck, you need to have the appropriate connection in place. For water, this means water-carrying pipes. For power, it means power lines. For garbage, it's a road, highway, rail, or Seaport connection. Road and rail connections each cost §2,500, highways cost §5,000. Seaports cost only the building fee. Water and power both require a §2,000 connection fee. There's no maximum number of connections, whether for pipes, wires, or transportation, but each one will cost you money. Moreover, additional connections make little or no functional difference in Neighbor Deals—one water main connected to your city's grid is just as effective at delivering or receiving water with a given neighbor as two or six or twelve connections would be. On the other hand, if your city is especially prone to disasters, maybe a little redundancy is in order…

FIG. 16-2. YOU HAVE TO MAKE A CONNECTION WITH YOUR NEIGHBOR BEFORE YOU CAN MAKE A DEAL WITH THEM.

Availability:

Your Utilities or Environmental Department advisor will tell you when a Neighbor Deal is possible and, if you don't have one already, encourage you to make the appropriate connection. (Whether or not you do this is entirely up to you, of course!) To be offered a deal, assuming the connection is in place, you must be using either 40 percent or less of the resource in question (for selling), or 80 percent or more (for buying).

FIG. 16-3. ADVISORS TELL YOU WHEN NEIGHBOR DEALS ARE POSSIBLE.

Duration:

Deal terms are checked every five years. However, if the terms of the deal do not need to change, the deal will continue as is, without notification. In a "sell" deal (where you are selling a service to a neighbor), the terms may change if, for instance, the neighbor's population has increased significantly and they need to buy a greater quantity of your service. On the other hand, if you are buying, the deal may remain the same if the original deal terms still satisfy your city's needs. If the terms are going to change, you will be notified six months before the end of the deal term, during which time you have the option of terminating the deal at no penalty or renewing at revised terms. If you do nothing at all, the new terms will be implemented and the deal will continue.

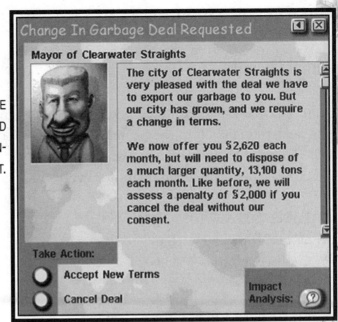

FIG. 16-4. YOU HAVE
SIX MONTHS BEFORE THE END
OF THE FIVE-YEAR NEIGHBOR DEAL CON-
TRACT TO DECIDE TO KEEP IT OR NOT.

Termination:

If you terminate the deal at any other time, either by bulldozing the connection or meeting with the Petitioner and ending the deal that way, you'll have to pay a penalty—possibly quite hefty. So unless you're really getting soaked (no pun intended), it's best to wait until a renegotiation period. Deals also can be terminated by the neighbor city if you can't live up to your end of the bargain and supply the agreed upon resource in the quantities required.

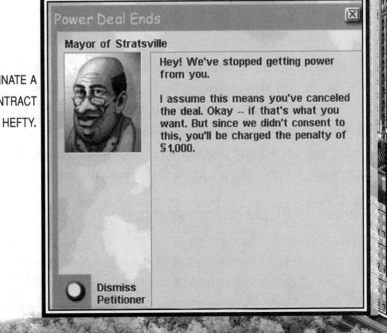

FIG. 16-5. IF YOU TERMINATE A
NEIGHBOR DEAL BEFORE THE CONTRACT
IS UP, THE FINES CAN BE HEFTY.

Sell Deals: Power, Water, and Garbage Disposal Capacity

Initial Quantity

Initial quantity is based on 20 percent of the neighbor's population at the time of the deal, rounded off to the nearest 1,000. So if Cray Town had a population of 10,000, the initial requirement would be to support 20 percent of the population, or 2,000. The quantity requirement for every 1,000 Sims is:

- Power: 500 Mw-h
- Water: 200 cubic meters
- Garbage: 65 tons

Sell Deal Initial Rate

The initial rate for a Neighbor Deal is based at §0.05 per unit for water and power and §0.50 per ton of garbage. The rate for water and power is actually quite high (resulting in lots of moolah for your treasury) because it only costs about §0.001 per unit to make power and §0.0007 per unit for water (equals the cost to plop down the building, divided by the units produced and modified by the expected life span).

Sell Deal Quantity and Rate Increases

Every five years the deal is reevaluated and a new rate may be offered, but only if the current deal is no longer sufficient to satisfy demand. The new quantity requested is equivalent to the percentage change in population of the neighbor. If the neighbor's population has increased by 20 percent, they will request a 20 percent increase in the purchase amount. If for some reason the population has not increased or decreased, the deal will remain as is.

Failure To Supply or Early Termination

Should you fail to deliver on a deal for any reason, you will have to cough up 10 times the monthly rate, regardless of the number of months left in the deal. This represents one-half of the total deal cost (because there are 60 months in the 5-year time span).

Buy Deals: Power, Water, and Garbage Disposal Capacity

Initial Quantity

The quantity purchased is equivalent to the need of the particular neighbor. If a deal exists for a particular resource, each neighbor connection of that resource is checked, and the required quantity will be provided. Because power and water are grid based, only those grids attached to the neighbor can receive the power or water. Garbage is global, so any connection to the neighbor will affect all garbage in the city. If your city doesn't need the extra capacity, only the minimum fee will apply.

However, when you enter a Neighbor Deal, you agree to purchase a certain capacity monthly, regardless of whether it's used or not. The guaranteed purchase amount is equivalent to the requirements of 10 percent of your city's population at the time of the deal, in multiples of 1,000. The quantity requirement for each 1,000 of population is:

- Power: 500 Mw-h
- Water: 200 cubic meters
- Garbage: 65 tons

Buy Deal Initial Rate

The initial rate for a Neighbor Deal is based at §0.05 per unit for water and power and §0.50 per ton of garbage. The rate for water and power is actually quite high (resulting in a serious drain on your treasury). Compare these numbers to the actual cost of about §0.001 per unit to make power and §0.0007 per unit for water (equals the cost to plop down the building, divided by the units produced and modified by the expected life span).

Buy Deal Quantity and Rate Increases

Deal terms are checked every five years. However, if the terms of the deal do not need to change, the deal will continue as is, without notification. If you are buying a service from a neighbor, the deal may remain the same if the original deal terms still satisfy your city's needs. If the terms are going to change, you will be notified six months before the end of the deal term, during which time you have the option of terminating the deal at no penalty or renewing at revised terms. If you do nothing at all, the new terms will be implemented and the deal will continue.

Early Termination

If you want to end the purchase deal before the end of its term, you will have to pay 10 times the monthly rate, regardless of the number of months left in the deal.

Strategy

In terms of strategy, Neighbor Deals can go either way. They can enable your city to weather various growth spurts and resource crises and grow to a major, thriving megalopolis. Or, you could end up with a repeat of the early 1970s oil crisis, when oil-producing nations had western countries literally over a barrel.

Fortunately, in *SimCity 3000*, your neighbors aren't looking to gouge you or to make a political statement. But you could find yourself in big trouble if you depend heavily on outside resources and can't meet the financial requirements as your demand goes up. Similarly, you can also have a major problem on your hands if your budget depends too much on Neighbor Deal income and their requirements go down, or if you can't meet increasing resource demands from your Neighbor Deals.

You can also have difficulties, although to a slightly lesser degree, if your neighbor has a baby boom and starts demanding more than you can deliver, forcing you to build more water pumps, power plants, or landfills. If the neighbor undergoes a growth spurt and you're their supplier, your infrastructure may not be able to handle the added load. Problems that could result include a lack of water to your own city, causing zones to degrade to low density; power overuse, resulting in power plants blowing up; or rampant garbage piling up everywhere. All of these impacts can cause land value losses throughout your city.

Similar problems can occur if your city grows rapidly, possibly requiring you to buy more resources, build more infrastructure, or stop selling the (now shrinking) excess.

The key word here is "dependence." To become truly dependent on Neighbor Deals to meet budgetary or resource needs can be very risky. Just ask those western countries. So let's be careful out there.

Water Deals

Water trading can give you money in exchange for extra water that you don't need, or provide badly needed water for your parched city. To have a water deal, you must make a water main connection to a neighbor, which costs §2,000 per connection.

You can't connect to a neighbor across water, though, and if you're entirely surrounded by water (like, uh, an island?) you can't have any water connections. Water, water everywhere, and not a drop to sell...

At any given time, you can have only two water deals active—one to buy water, one to sell—even though it's possible you could have multiple water connections with as many as four neighbors. Any water connections not being used for a water exchange deal just sit there doing nothing at all. Clearly, the only point in building a water connection and forking over that §2,000 fee is if you actually plan to use the thing.

You can see the status of any water connection in the Neighbor window. To cancel or negotiate a deal, you must meet with a Petitioner, from the Meet Petitioner list. If you already have a deal, a Petitioner is always available, both through the Meet Petitioner list and the "Adjust Deal" button in the Neighbor window—consider it your own personal contact from your neighbor city's Mayor's office. For an existing deal, the Petitioner describes the terms and penalty for early termination, or if new terms are being negotiated, offers you the chance to back out at no penalty.

Selling Water

You can make lots of money selling water to a thirsty neighbor city. On the other hand, increasing water demands from the neighbor can force you to create a much larger water infrastructure than you'd normally need and raises the risk of water shortages and penalty fees if you're unable to meet their needs.

You can be offered a deal (through a Petitioner) to sell water if the following conditions are met:

- A water connection is available to a neighbor city and it isn't being used currently to buy water.
- You're using 40 percent or less of your water capacity.
- Your water main connecting to the neighbor is receiving water from some
- source.
- You aren't currently selling water to anyone else.
  No other Petitioners are offering to sell you water.

If you opt to enter into a water-selling deal, you must supply a certain amount of water each month to that neighbor. The amount needed is initially determined by a number of gallons, multiplied by the neighbor's population, and that amount is updated every five years. The amount you receive is a certain number of Simoleons per gallon, multiplied by your population.

Your city's water infrastructure shows no particular preference for meeting either your or your neighbor's needs. If the water supply is inadequate, your own city buildings' water spigots have as much chance of going dry as your neighbor's.

If you terminate the water connection before the end of a contract term, you'll have to cough up a penalty fee, based on a percentage of the current rate. The deal itself is considered terminated if any of the following occur:

- The neighbor can't get enough water because of inadequate supply on your part.
- The water main representing the connection isn't receiving water from your water grid.
- You destroy the water line representing the connection (or anywhere along the path connecting to the water main, such that there's no alternate route).
- You cancel the deal through the Petitioner at a time when the deal isn't being renegotiated.

You can get a current status on the deal either through the Neighbor window or by using the Query tool on the water connection itself.

Buying Water

You can get as much water as you could ever need by buying water from a neighbor. This reduces the risk of running short and having your city turn into a latter-day dustbowl, plus it reduces somewhat the need to worry about water pollution. However, as you and your neighbor cities grow, increasing both the amount of water you need and the price you have to pay to get it, the financial burden could flush your budget right down the, uh, you know.

You can be offered a deal to buy water if:

- There's a water connection available, and the neighbor to which it's connected isn't already buying or selling water with you through it.
- You are using 80 percent or more of the capacity of your current water system.
- You aren't currently buying water from any other neighbor.
- No Petitioners are currently offering to buy water from you.

Water buying supplies a varying amount of water, depending on your city's needs. When the connection is in place and the deal agreed upon, the water connection behaves as if a water plant were there at the point of connection, with unlimited supply. To make use of the water, your buildings need to be on the grid with the supply connection. A city can have multiple water grids and for water to reach any given zone, there has to be an unbroken line of pipes from the neighbor connection to within six tiles of it.

Now, your water utility managers are smart enough not to buy water if you have enough on hand to supply your city through your own pumping systems. On the other hand, these water buying deals do specify a minimum fee, even if you don't use any neighbor-supplied water, so it's best not to have a water deal unless you need one.

Water deals operate on a monthly basis. At the end of each month, the required amount of water is purchased from the neighbor and the corresponding amount of funds is deducted from your treasury.

Because a water purchase is considered an operating budget expenditure, the treasury can drop below zero to keep paying for your Sims' imported water.

Periodically, the deal may be reevaluated. News of any updates to the deal will be available for six months before the price change takes place, giving you an opportunity to back out of the deal with no penalty. If you terminate the deal at any other time, either explicitly through the Petitioner window or implicitly by destroying the water connection, you're charged a stiff fee. When new terms are being offered, they will go into effect automatically if you do nothing during the six-month renegotiation period.

Power Deals

Power trading works just about the same as for water. A power deal can give you money in exchange for extra electricity that you don't need, or provide badly needed energy for your power-hungry city. To have a power deal, you must make a high-tension power line connection to a neighbor, which costs §2,000 per connection.

Because you have a maximum of four neighbors, that's the largest number of connections you can have. You can't connect to a neighbor across water, though, and if your city is on an island and completely surrounded by ocean, you can't have any neighbor power connections.

At any time, you can have only two power deals active—one to buy power, one to sell—even though it's possible you could have up to four power connections. These unused connections, and any other power connection not being used for a deal, just sit there. It's best to build a connection and pay that §2,000 fee only if you actually plan to use it.

You can see the status of any power connection in the Neighbor window. To cancel or negotiate a deal, you must meet with a Petitioner, from the Meet Petitioner list. If you already have a deal, a Petitioner is always available, both through the Meet Petitioner list and the "Adjust Deal" button in the Neighbor window. For an existing deal, the Petitioner describes the terms and penalty for early termination, or if new terms are being negotiated, offers you the chance to back out at no penalty.

Selling Power

You can make pretty decent money selling power to a neighbor city. On the other hand, increasing power demands from the neighbor can force you to create a much larger power infrastructure than you'd normally need and raises the risk of blackouts and penalty fees if you're unable to meet their needs. In addition, if you overtax, your power plants there is a good possibility that they will blow up. Not good.

You can be offered a deal (through a Petitioner) to sell power if the following conditions are met:

- A power connection is available to a neighbor city and it isn't being used currently to buy power.
- You are using 40 percent or less of your power capacity.
- Your line connecting to the neighbor is receiving power from some source.
- You aren't currently selling power to anyone else.
- No other Petitioners are offering to sell you power.

If you decide to enter into a power-selling deal, you must supply a certain amount of power each month to that neighbor.

Your city's power grid shows no particular preference for meeting either yours or your neighbor's needs. If the power supply is inadequate, your own city buildings are just as prone to blackouts as your neighbor's.

Periodically, both the rate and amount purchased may be renegotiated.

If you terminate the power connection, you'll have to pay a penalty fee, based on a percentage of the current rate. The deal itself is considered terminated if any of the following occurs:

- The neighbor can't get enough power because of an inadequate supply on your part.
- The high-tension power line representing the connection isn't receiving power from your grid.
- You destroy the power line representing the connection (or anywhere along the path to the connection, such that there's no alternate route).
- You cancel the deal through the Petitioner at a time when the deal isn't being renegotiated.

You can get a current status on the deal either through the Neighbor window or by using the Query tool on the power connection itself.

Buying Power

You can get as much power as you need by buying it from a neighbor. This reduces the risk of running short, plus reduces somewhat the need to worry about power plant capacity limits. However, as you and your neighbor cities grow, increasing both the amount of power you need and the price you have to pay to get it, the financial burden could fry your poor city.

You can be offered a deal to buy power if:

- There's a power connection available, and the neighbor to which it's connected isn't already buying or selling power with you through it.
- You're using 80 percent or more of the capacity of your current power grid.
- You aren't currently buying power from any other neighbor.
- No Petitioners are currently offering to buy power from you.

Buying power supplies a varying amount of electricity, depending on your city's needs. When the connection is in place and the deal agreed upon, the power connection behaves as if there's a power plant at the point of connection, with unlimited supply. To make use of the power, your buildings need to be on the grid with the supply connection.

Your power utility managers know not to buy power if you have enough on hand to supply your city through your own power systems, without running your plants at overcapacity. On the other hand, power-buying deals do specify a minimum fee, even if you don't use any neighbor-supplied power, so it's best not to have a power deal unless you need one.

Power deals operate on monthly basis. At the end of each month, the required amount of power is purchased from the neighbor and the corresponding amount of funds is deducted from your treasury.

Because buying power is considered an operating budget expenditure, the treasury can drop below zero to keep paying for your Sims' imported power.

Periodically, the deal may be reevaluated. News of the update will be available for six months before the price change takes place, giving you an opportunity to back out of the deal with no penalty. If you terminate the deal at any other time, either explicitly through the Petitioner window or implicitly by destroying the power connection, you're charged a stiff fee. If you do nothing when new rates are offered, the new deal will go into effect automatically at the end of the six-month renegotiation period.

Garbage Deals

Here we go again. Garbage deals work very much like water or power deals. However, there are a few differences between garbage deals and the other kinds:

- The connection to your neighbor to export or import garbage can be over road, rail, or Seaport. Road and rail connections cost §2,500, highway connections are §5,000. All supply benefits to your city.
- Because a Seaport is a valid connection for handling garbage, your city can still import or export garbage, even if you're on an island.
- There's no minimum fee if you don't need to export garbage for a given month when you have a garbage export deal.

It might seem a little confusing at first—you pay money to get water or power from a neighbor city, but *they* pay *you* to take their refuse. A mental model that can make this easier is if you think in terms of *garbage capacity*. What they're actually paying for is the limited resource of a city's garbage-handling capabilities. They're paying you for space in your landfills or incinerators, if you're importing their garbage, or you're paying them for theirs, if you're exporting refuse.

At any given time, you can have only two garbage deals active—one to import garbage, one to export.

You can see the status of any garbage deal in the Neighbor Map window. To cancel or negotiate a deal, you must meet with a Petitioner, from the Meet Petitioner list. If you already have a deal, a Petitioner is always available, both through the Meet Petitioner list and the "Adjust Deal" button in the Neighbor window. For an existing deal, the Petitioner describes the terms and penalty for early termination, or if new terms are being negotiated, offers you the chance to back out at no penalty.

Importing Garbage

There's money in trash. Lots of it. On the other hand, rising garbage-handling demands from the neighbor can force you to create huge landfills and build incinerators by the six-pack. If you start turning back their garbage trucks or barges, the penalty fees run high. If the situation gets bad enough, trash will start to accumulate in your city, slowly burying it until all your Sims flee like rats off a stinking…uh, sinking ship.

You can be offered a deal (through a Petitioner) to import garbage if the following conditions are met:

- A road, highway rail, or Seaport is available to a neighbor city and it's not being used currently to import trash.
- You're using 40 percent or less of your garbage-handling capacity.
- You have roads or rails linking the connection point(s) to your landfill(s) and incinerator(s).
- You aren't currently importing garbage from anyone else.
- No other Petitioners are offering to send you their trash.

If you decide to enter into a garbage import deal, you must accept a certain amount of garbage each month from that neighbor. The amount imported is determined initially by a number of kilotons, multiplied by the neighbor's population, and that amount is updated every five years. The amount you receive is a certain number of Simoleons per kiloton, multiplied by your population, divided into equal portions for each month the deal is in effect.

Garbage disposal operates on a priority basis, with imported garbage at the top of the proverbial heap. The following is the order in which your city's sanitation engineers pick up and process refuse, assuming your city has the capacity to handle it:

Garbage imported from a neighbor
Citywide monthly garbage output
Accumulated garbage piles in the city

Garbage disposal also uses a priority system to determine where trash goes first:

Waste-to-Energy plant(s)
Incinerator(s)
Local landfill(s)
Export via a Neighbor Deal

If the garbage capacity is inadequate, both your and your neighbor's cities will soon be awash with refuse (although the only trash you'll actually see will be in your own city). If you don't fix this problem quickly, the neighbor's Petitioner will show up to cancel the deal and charge a penalty.

Periodically, both the rate and amount imported may be renegotiated.

If you terminate the transport connection, you'll have to pay a penalty fee, based on a percentage of the current rate. The deal itself is considered terminated if any of the following occur:

- The road, highway, rail, or Seaport system won't allow trash to reach the landfill or incinerators.
- You destroy the road, highway, rail, or Seaport representing the connection.
- You cancel the deal through the Petitioner at a time when the deal isn't being renegotiated.

You can get a current status on the deal through the Neighbor window.

Exporting Garbage

Go ahead—let someone else deal with your city's garbage. The benefits of this can seem staggering: No unsightly landfills. No smoke-belching incinerators. More high-value land on which to grow your city.

Ah, but it would be a perfect arrangement, if not for the fact that as your neighbor's population grows, they'll charge you more and more for taking your garbage. Like you, they don't want immense landfills crowding their nice clean cities.

And there's that nagging little problem of conscience. Some Mayors, believe it or not, still have one, and the idea of shipping their garbage out for someone else to deal with can be acutely uncomfortable. For some Mayors, anyway.

If you do manage to get past this quandary, the garbage export deal is there. Once you have a deal, you can export as much garbage as you need to—whatever excess can't be handled by your own landfills or incinerators, assuming you have any.

You can be offered a deal to export garbage if:

- There's a road, highway, rail, or Seaport connection available, and the neighbor to which it's connected isn't already importing or exporting garbage with you through it.
- You are using 80 percent or more of your garbage-handling capacity.
- You aren't currently exporting garbage to any other neighbor.
- No Petitioners are currently offering to send their garbage to you.

Your garbage workers—sorry, refuse-handling engineers—know not to export garbage if you have enough local handling capacity. Besides, they really don't feel like traveling all the way to the next city if there's a place nearby that can take their loads.

Garbage deals operate on monthly basis. At the end of each month, the required amount of garbage is exported to the neighbor and the corresponding amount of funds is deducted from your treasury.

Because it's considered an operating budget expenditure, the treasury can drop below zero to keep paying for garbage export.

Periodically, the deal may be reevaluated and a new price is set. News of the update will be available for six months before the price change takes place, giving you an opportunity to back out of the deal with no penalty. If you terminate the deal at any other time, either explicitly through the Petitioner window or implicitly by destroying the road, highway, rail, or Seaport connection, you're charged a penalty. If you do nothing when new rates are offered, the new deal will go into effect automatically at the end of the six-month renegotiation period.

Neighbor and SimNation Populations

The most important thing to realize about neighbor and SimNation populations is that neither have any effect on the RCI demand of your city. Your city's growth isn't dependent on the growth of your neighbors or SimNation.

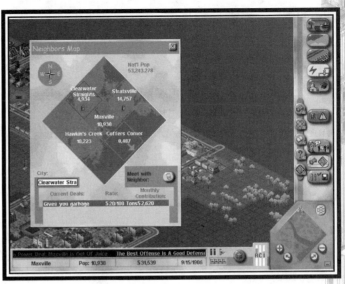

FIG. 16-6. FROM THE NEIGHBOR MAP, YOU CAN SEE POPULATION FIGURES FOR YOUR OWN CITY, YOUR NEIGHBOR CITIES, AND SIMNATION.

Neighbor Population

- At the start of a new city, each neighbor's population is set randomly between 2,000 and 15,000.
- Each year their population will change by a random percentage between –5 percent and +10 percent.
- Neighbor populations are capped at four million, and then fluctuate randomly around that amount.
- SimNation population will be approximately 0.8 percent annually.
- Connections with neighbors and neighbor deals have no effect on neighbor populations.

SimNation Population

At the start of a new game, the population of SimNation is set to the combined population of your city and your neighbors times 1,500.

Each year, the SimNation population will increase by approximately 0.8 percent. SimNation population is capped at one billion, and then fluctuates randomly around that amount.

Chapter 17
Business Deals

Aside from taxes, ordinances, and Neighbor Deals, another potential source of revenue for your city is the Business Deal. Unlike Neighbor Deals, these don't depend on a connection to other cities to happen. Essentially, a person shows up at your mayoral office, offering a proposal: "You build this here and we'll see to it you're rewarded handsomely … "

Of course, being the clever Mayor you are, you're sure to suspect something's up. Your suspicions are well founded.

In reality, you're being offered a monthly payment in exchange for putting up a seriously NIMBY building of some sort or other. Furthermore, you'll likely have to deal with increased pollution and garbage, and suffer losses in overall land value in the areas near these buildings.

If you agree to the deal, you'll then be able to construct the requested building, although there's no set time limit for doing this. Of course, the payments only start after you've plopped the building. You can only place the Business Deal building after it has been offered, and you can have only one of each type in your city at any given time.

You have the option of locating the building way off in some corner of your city to help minimize the negative effects, but it's worth noting that it must tie into successful trip generation, be supplied with utilities, and so on, for you to continue receiving the monthly bribe … er, compensation.

So the big question is, do you accept the deal or don't you? That *is* the question. We'll get to that in a minute. In the meantime, here are some details about Business Deals in general.

Getting a Business Deal

Business deals are random events, triggered starting in 1915, if:

- You have less than three years' operating expenses on hand, at current spending levels, *and*
- More than three years have passed since you were last offered a Business Deal, *and*
- More than five years have passed since you last terminated a Business Deal

FIG. 17-1. FROM HERE, YOU CAN SEE THE SUMMARY OF ANY CONTRIBUTION TO YOUR BUDGET FROM BUSINESS DEALS.

The income generated from your Business Deals is displayed in the Income Budget window. Clicking on the Business Deals "Meet Advisor" button takes you to your Financial Advisor's briefing on the subject. If you click on the "Adjust" button instead, it takes you to the Business Deals window; from there, you can also get to your Financial Advisor.

FIG. 17-2. THIS WINDOW SHOWS YOU THE MONTHLY REVENUE COMING FROM ANY BUSINESS DEALS YOU MIGHT HAVE.

Business deals are offered by petitioners, and you receive notification of the option both through the news ticker and the Meet Petitioner window.

Types of Business Deals

There are four kinds of business deal buildings:

TABLE 17-1. EFFECTS OF BUSINESS DEALS

Building	Monthly Tax Benefit	Negative Effects
Toxic Waste Factory	§400/month	pollution, land value
Maximum Security Prison	§250/month	land value
MegaMall	§300/month	pollution, land value, drastic reduction in Commercial demand
Casino	§350/month	crime, pollution

FIG. 17-3. TOXIC WASTE
FACTORY, MAXIMUM SECURITY
PRISON, MEGAMALL,
AND CASINO.

Following is a breakdown of exactly how bad the negative effects are:

TABLE 17-2. DETRIMENTAL EFFECTS OF BUSINESS DEAL BUILDINGS

Building	Garbage	Water Pollution	Air Pollution	Residential Land Value	Commercial Land Value	Industrial Land Value
Toxic Waste Factory	+60	+500	+7,000	-§90,000	-§50,000	-§30,000
Maximum Security Prison	+144	+70	+70	-§40,000	-§20,000	-§10,000
MegaMall	+144	+80	+60	-§10,000	-§15,000	N/A
Casino	+144	+60	+60	-§40,000	+§15,000	-§15,000

Terminating Business Deals

Killing an existing business deal is actually quite simple: Demolish the building.
Doing this will remove the deal from the list of Business Deals, and obviously, the
bribe … er, revenue stream, stops immediately.

NIMBY Range

Each of the Business Deals buildings are 5 x 5 tiles in size, with their NIMBY range radiating several tiles in every direction, although with gradually decreasing effect.

Do I or Don't I?

This has been the question on which we went round and round. Should we be good little Mayors and turn down these nefarious Business Deals? Or should we give in to temptation? Let's look at the pros and cons.

The Pros:

- You get a pretty decent and steady monthly income from these buildings. (For example, there's a reason why Nevada has no state income tax. Think about it.)
- The graphics for these Business Deal buildings are cool.
- They add to the complexity and entertainment value of your city.

The Cons:

- The garbage, pollution, and land value hits can be rather severe for all the buildings.
- The Casino generates a lot of crime.
- The MegaMall drastically reduces Commercial demand.
- Nobody wants to live anywhere near a Toxic Waste Factory or a Maximum Security Prison.

The conclusion? Take the money and run.

No, really! It turns out there are things you can do to alleviate the worst of the problems for each type of building, while at the same time making use of this nifty feature into which the Maxis developers put a lot of effort. Following are a few tricks you can use:

Toxic Waste Factory: Locate this way out at the edge of your city map. Like, right on the edge. This will cut the pollution almost in half. Also, because it's out at the edge, your city won't suffer as badly from the land value reduction. To alleviate the air and water pollution, plant trees and build a Water Treatment Plant nearby; the trees also will help a little with the land value. For the garbage production, you may consider locating a landfill or a Waste-to-Energy Incinerator there as well.

Maximum Security Prison: The biggest hit on this one is the land value. Pollution and garbage are more manageable. Like the Toxic Waste Factory, the best place for the prison is out at the edge of your city map. Don't be afraid to locate this one on your least attractive territory. One thing you won't have to worry about is any increase in crime—when they say *Maximum Security* Prison, they mean it. Nobody gets out of this facility until their sentence is up.

MegaMall: This one's kind of tricky. It produces more pollution than the Maximum Security Prison and Casino, but less than the Toxic Waste Factory. The land value reduction is the least of all the Business Deal buildings. The worst effect of the MegaMall is that it drastically reduces Commercial demand. On top of this, to keep from completely trashing your Commercial tax income, you need the MegaMall to do reasonably well as a business, so locating it out at the edge of the map isn't a terribly good idea. Still, that's an option, as long as you have a good transportation system to allow Sims to get there. Another possible solution is to put the MegaMall a short distance away from your Commercial district(s), and maybe surround it with parks and other facilities designed to raise land value. It's probably not a good idea to put it too close to your City Center, however. To help with the Commercial demand reduction, consider lowering the Commercial tax rate a point or two, or pass ordinances to encourage Commercial growth.

Casino: Okay, this leads to relatively moderate problems with garbage and pollution; you already know how to handle these. The land value reduction, worse than for the MegaMall, but not as bad as for the Toxic Waste Factory or the Maximum Security Prison. Because the worst problem with the Casino is crime, we recommend that you plop the building wherever you want (although well away from your City Center is best). Then, drop one or two police stations right alongside the Casino. The "Sims In Blue" will do their duty to keep the more nefarious elements at bay.

   In summary, what we're saying here is that although these Business Deal buildings have their problems, they're nothing you, the skilled and enlightened Mayor, can't handle. So go ahead and build 'em when they're offered!

Chapter 18
Triggered and Threshold Events

As the years go by and your city grows, certain events occur. These events come in two types:

* Time triggered events
* Milestone rewards

The first type, time-triggered events, occur on or around a specific year in game play, and usually involve the availability of a new kind of building or structure. They're different from other time-dependent events, such as when new ordinances become available.

The second, milestone rewards, are buildings you're given access to build upon achieving certain goals. These are your Sims' way of saying, "All right, Mayor! Hurrah!"

Time-Triggered Events

These events are advances in power, water, garbage, and transit systems:

TABLE 18-1. IMPORTANT SIMCITY DATES

Building	Year Available	Cost	Output/Effect
Subway Station	1910	§500	Enables building of subway system
Airport	1930	§500/tile	Enables air travel (commerce and industry benefit)
Incinerator	1920	§7,500	Burns up to 4,500 kilotons of trash per month, converting it into air pollution (cough!)
Bus Station	1920	§150	Helps reduce traffic
Water Treatment Plant	1935	§15,000	Reduces water pollution levels, increasing the efficiency of your water supply system
Highways	1940	§600/block	Handles four times the traffic capacity of normal two-lane road Cheaper after 1965
Gas Power Plant	1955	§4,500	Provides 3,000 MW-h/month relatively clean power, but is expensive
Water Desalinization Plant	1960	§1,000	Provides water for your Sims, must be placed next to ocean shore or it won't work
Nuclear Power Plant	1960	§20,000	Provides 1,600 MW-h/month of clean power (not available if you select Nuclear Free Zone Ordinance); there's a risk of major nasty nuclear meltdown and your very own Chernobyl if you push the plant beyond 100 percent capacity
Recycling Center	1970	§5,000	Usage/population
Wind Generator	1980	§250	Provides 200 MW-h/month of clean power; works best high up on hills
Solar Generator	1985	§15,000	Provides 5,000 MW-h/month of clean, eco-friendly power (works best in sunny climates, of course)
Waste-to-Energy Incinerator	2000	§25,000	Converts up to 5,250 kilotons of garbage per month into power, but does produce a lot of air pollution and reduces land values
Microwave Power Plant	2020	§30,000	14,000 MW-h/month of clean power
Fusion Power Plant	2050	§50,000	50,000 MW-h/month of clean power, thanks to science!

Milestone Rewards

Besides letting you feel smug and satisfied with the job you've been doing as Mayor of your city, these reward buildings sometimes have additional side benefits:

TABLE 18-2. MILESTONE REWARDS

Building	Milestone
Mayor's House	Population at 5,000
City Hall	Population at 20,000
County Courthouse	Population at 25,000
National Park	> 35 park tiles in city
Statue	Population at 35,000
Lighthouse	Population at 15,000
Country Club	Population at 125,000
Military Base	Population at 80,000
Medical Institute	Population at 80,000, Date > 1999
Science Center	EQ > 135, Date > 1999
Arts Center	Population at 100,000
University	EQ > 105
Theme Park	Population at 80,000
Defense Contractor	Military Base in city
Stock Exchange	Population at 200,000, treasury level > §50,000
Spaceport	Population at 350,000, Airport at 50 fully devoloped tiles, Date>2050

TABLE 18-3. AWARD BUILDING EFFECTS ON LAND VALUE

Building	Residential	Commercial	Industrial	Non-RCI Zoned
Mayor's House	23	20	2	2
City Hall	20	25	N/A	N/A
County Courthouse	20	25	N/A	N/A
Geyser Park	5	15	5	5
Statue	18	18	5	4
Lighthouse	12	25	0	0
Country Club	35	7	5	5
Military Base	-20	12	12	-8
Medical Institute	5	5	5	5
Science Center	10	10	N/A	N/A
Arts Center	12	20	0	0
University	5	15	0	0
Theme Park	-18	12	0	0
Defense Contractor	-20	18	12	-8
Stock Exchange	-5	35	-4	0
Spaceport	-30	-25	10	0

Chapter 19
Puttin' It All Together

All right. Now you're familiar with each of the distinct elements that make *SimCity 3000* tick. You've got a firm grasp of the workings of RCI and the effect of land values on building development and taxes, what causes population to grow or shrink, how to handle your budget, what the different ordinances do, and the various effects of power, water, transportation, and city services. You're ready for the challenges of being the *Mayor*!

Yours will be the guiding philosophy that takes your city toward its ultimate destiny as a thriving metropolis, a pleasant suburban town, or even a pastoral landscape prized by a few happy Sims. Most of our emphasis in this book has been to help you to understand the workings of *SimCity 3000* and how to maximize population, land values, and overall city size and quality. However, with a thorough understanding of how things work in your city, you can determine its direction and have a reasonable degree of control over the kind of city you create.

What Do You Want To Build Today?

FIG. 19-1. *SIMCITY 3000* LETS YOU BUILD HUGE CITIES WITH THRIVING CITY CENTERS.

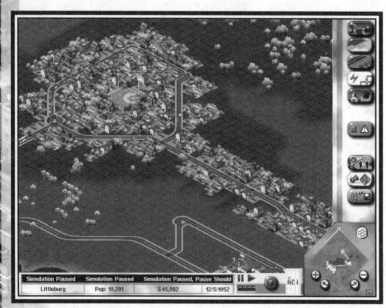

FIG. 19-2. YOU CAN ALSO CREATE MORE MODEST CITIES.

FIG. 19-4. THE TERRAIN MAP OF SAN FRANCISCO WAS MADE USING IMPORTED BUMP MAPS FROM THE USGS. SEE APPENDIX A FOR MORE INFORMATION.

FIG. 19-3. YOU CAN EVEN BUILD A FARM COMMUNITY.

The way *SimCity 3000* operates, it may seem that the only city you can build is a huge megalopolis—always striving to be bigger and more densely populated. To be honest, there are some aspects of the simulation engine that tend to promote a large and expanding city with a very dense Commercial City Center. However, you can build a successful, solvent city with other schemes. For instance, it's possible to build a city entirely with low-density zoning and still be financially solvent. Such a city will look very different from the huge metropolis. And that's one of the beauties of *SimCity 3000*. Because of the great detail in the graphics for this simulation, cities really do take on a specific look based on how you manage them. We won't tell you what kind of city to build, but we encourage experimentation. Try different city plans and visions. Create a suburban sprawl or a city of strip malls. Create a country town, or even a group of individual small communities separated by lakes, rivers, or mountains, perhaps. Use your imagination, because, chances are, you'll see many unique results if you do.

In the rest of this chapter, we'll attempt to put all the pieces into perspective by providing a practical look at *SimCity* from a different angle. First, it's important to understand how *SimCity* operates.

Taking Turns

Even though your cities seem to live in some form of continuous SimTime, *SimCity 3000* actually works by rechecking certain internal values in definable turns. These turns, for the most part, relate to months of SimTime. So, in essence, every month is a milestone. One of the keys to success in *SimCity 3000* is to be aware of the same information that the simulation is using. By integrating the various "layers" of information into one overall viewpoint, you can improve your chances of accomplishing your *SimCity 3000* goals.

The Mayor as Pilot

Once you've grasped each of the individual elements that affect your city, you can begin to understand the kinds of information you must track on a monthly and yearly basis. Now, you could just wing it, but you can also take a hint from the way a pilot flies an airplane—by creating a checklist of tasks to perform or information to monitor on a regular basis.

When flying a plane, or even when driving a car, it's important to monitor certain conditions and information on a regular and repetitive basis. In the simplest example, a pilot always checks the plane's altitude regularly and checks the radar periodically for low-flying UFOs. A driver should always check in the rear-view mirror, monitor the vehicle's speed, and even cast an eye on the gas and temperature gauges from time to time. In *SimCity*, there are also a number elements to track and to keep tracking. These include such aspects as the relative demand for Residential, Commercial, and Industrial(RCI) development, the current budget, and even the distribution of water through your city, just to name a few.

Cross Section

Let's try freezing a city in time and seeing what's going on. We'll take a cross-section view of the "layers" of this city and, from that, we'll begin to see what we have to be aware of.

Global RCI demand is the fundamental force that is driving the development of your city.

Power makes everything go.

Water is necessary for high-density development and land values, and also for reducing the risk of fire.

Transportation is a complex layer that affects whether Sims can get to and from their destinations. Transportation can be subdivided into two distinct categories: roads of various kinds and mass transit.

Pollution is a result of industry and traffic, but mostly industry. Other things, including Commercial and Residential development, also produce a small but measurable amount of pollution. Pollution is inevitable, but must be minimized and monitored.

Your city produces trash, which can build up and lower land values if not properly disposed of. The amount of garbage must be monitored.

City growth will be stifled if there aren't enough connections outside the city, so neighbor connections, Airports, and Seaports must be built and expanded as your city grows.

Crime is a real danger to your city's growth, so police coverage must be monitored.

Fire can destroy whole cities if left unchecked, so fire coverage must be monitored. (Even if you have Disasters turned off, your Sims will still demand Fire Departments.)

Your city's residents won't live to ripe old ages if their health care is not provided, so be sure you've provided adequate hospital coverage and have passed health-promoting ordinances.

- Your city won't develop to its fullest potential if its residents aren't given a good education, so schools and colleges must be built and their effectiveness monitored.
- Sims will begin to lose their educational edge if they have no way to remain stimulated, so libraries and museums must be provided and the amount of their coverage monitored.
- Sims will only tolerate a dull, boring city so long before they demand some recreation. So stadiums, parks, and other entertainment venues must be provided to keep the Sims happy and the city growing.
- Your city runs not only on power and water, but on money as well. And all these wonderful city services you're providing are costing you. You must continually be aware of your budget—not only the bottom line, but the specifics of taxation and departmental funding.
- Ordinances are one way you can affect your city's development, the quality of life in your city, and, in some cases, the flow of cash in your budget. You need to be aware of the effect of different ordinances when they become available. Because each ordinance has a cost and a benefit, you must periodically weigh the cost-to-benefit ratio to see if the ordinance should be enacted or cancelled at any given time.
- Periodically, you'll want to assess the possibility of a power, water, or garbage trading deal with a neighbor. If you have deals in place, you'll want to monitor them carefully, as they can have a significant effect on your city—and not always a positive or desirable one.
- Periodically, you may be offered a special Business Deal. You'll want to know the state of your city when the deal is offered and how it might affect your long-range goals. If you have a Business Deal in place, assess it periodically to see if it's still providing what your city needs or if it's no longer useful.
- One of the best ways to tune into your city's needs is to watch the news tickers and check in periodically with your city's advisors and the various Petitioners. Petitioners are especially informative because they represent the voice of your SimPopulation. Of course, just because some overzealous Sim is demanding action of you doesn't mean you have to take that action. You're still the Mayor. It's always your decision in the end.

Whew! Who said running a city was easy?

How To Make Intelligent SimDecisions

Now that we've reflected on the many factors that affect the growth of your city, let's look at how you might monitor those factors so you can make the best decisions. What follows is a suggested checklist for the Mayor's city management duties:

Check RCI demand: You should watch the rise and fall of demand for Residential, Commercial, and Industrial land like a hawk. Although you don't want to overbuild, your city will only grow if you provide zoned land for development. There's often a delay between the time you create new zoned areas and the resulting effect on RCI demand.

- Watch news tickers and keep an eye out for anything unusual.
- Check periodically for new Petitioners and see what they're saying.

When in doubt, see what your city's advisors are recommending.

- Check your budget: You want always to be aware of available funds, cash flow (plus or minus), and end-of-year totals. For instance, if you have §2,000 cash available, but your end-of-year balance will be §5, you have a negative §1995 cash flow for the year and, unless you can generate some revenue or cut spending, you'll soon be broke.

Do some spot checks for crime density versus police and fire coverage. Make sure your city is a safe place to live, because that will promote higher land values, which, in turn, will provide higher taxes, and should also attract more Sims to your city.

Likewise, make sure you have enough educational buildings and health care for your population. Check that you're allocating enough money to these departments in your budget. Query buildings like schools, colleges, and hospitals to see check their performance "grade," which will be an A+ through an F.

Be sure your water system is providing water to every building; land development is severely limited where there's no water.

Check the amount of pollution in your water system. Pollution will severely reduce the effectiveness of your various water sources.

Check your landfills or incinerators and make sure they're still operating under capacity.

Every so often, especially when your city is growing fast, check your power plant to be sure it isn't operating above 100 percent capacity. If it's near or above 100 percent, it's time to build a second plant or buy power from a neighbor if you've got money to burn. Running a power plant over its capacity is a sure-fire way to make it explode.

- Look at the buildings in your city. Do they look seedy and run down? Are there many vacant lots? If so, you need to do something to raise land values.
- Check pollution levels from time to time.
- Occasionally query individual buildings and zones. Pay particular attention to land values and pollution levels, and keep a close eye on your utilities like power plants and Water Pumps, which have fixed lifetimes and can start to deteriorate over time.
- Use the various maps and charts to see the bigger picture of your city, and use the information from those maps and charts to identify trends and trouble areas.

Troubleshooting

How To Have a Healthy Budget

If you find yourself in need of cash—an entirely common mayoral experience— there are several steps you can take, some direct and some more indirect.

Direct Methods

The following actions can directly affect your budget's bottom line, leaving you with more money at the end of the year:

Raise taxes: Never a popular decision, this will certainly affect how your resident Sims view you and can slow city growth if you raise taxes too high. As a city grows larger, its sensitivity to higher taxes increases, so be careful with tax raises in a mature city.

Take out a loan: You can raise immediate money by taking out a loan, but you'll be paying for it over the next 10 years. It's a good idea to have a plan when going into debt. Be sure that you can invest the new money wisely and that it will pay dividends in the end.

Reduce spending: Sometimes you can find ways to cut back on spending. There are various risks and rewards for doing so. Some possible methods for cutting spending:

- Cut departmental spending: There are risks to this. First of all, services will most likely degrade and affect your city in other ways. For instance, cutting funding to the police station will most likely result in an increase in crime, which in turn will lower land values, which in turn will lower taxes. Cutting funding to other departments can have different, but similarly damaging effects. And there's always the danger of a strike when you cut funding to any department.

- Reduce infrastructure: It may be that you've created redundancy in some area or other. For instance, you may have built far too many roads. Replacing some roads with small parks could increase land values and lower Transportation Department expenses, though the effect would not be large. But, if you have extra hospitals or Fire Departments, for instance, bulldozing one or two of them could reduce your yearly budget by a noticeable amount.

- Repeal or enact ordinances: Some ordinances cost you money, while others will produce more for the city's coffers. In times of financial need, you can affect your bottom line by using ordinances. For more specific information, read Chapter 15.

- Make a Neighbor Deal: Sometimes a good deal with a neighbor can bail you out of financial trouble in a hurry. Examine the terms before signing on the dotted line, and if they work for you, go for it!

- Make a Business Deal: Periodically, you'll receive an offer from an outside party interested in building in your city. Business deals always bring in more money, but they also always have some undesirable side effects. Read the chapter on Business Deals for more information about them.

Indirect Methods

There are other ways to increase your Simoleon intake:

Increase Land Values: This is one of the prime methods for improving your city's fiscal health. However, improving land values is always a result of other actions you take, like reducing pollution and eliminating trash buildup, building parks and other land-improving structures, providing better transportation, and reducing crime. Remember that fulfilling demand for one type of zone will create additional demand for other types. A healthy Industrial sector will create demand for more Residential, and a growing Residential sector creates demand for both Industrial and Commercial.

Build or expand Airports and Seaports: One way to increase the flow of supply and demand in your city is to be sure that you have adequate connections to the outside world. Sometimes a city needs to expand, and, at certain population thresholds, Airports and Seaports must be expanded for the city to continue its growth trend. However, don't overexpand. Airports and Seaports carry heavy costs with them—they don't pay taxes, they produce high pollution and crime, and they use a lot of power and water. Expand these facilities slowly as your city's population grows, especially if your Industrial or Commercial demand seems to be flagging and other measures are ineffective. (Also, see the notes on RCI caps below.)

Build new neighbor connections: Neighbor connections stimulate new business and demand, so a new connection can sometimes give a stagnant economy a boost.

Promoting City Growth

Cities can become stagnant for various reasons. There are two major reasons why a city might not continue growing:

- If certain demand caps are reached
- If the city isn't a desirable place to live and work

Demand caps act as restrictions to a city's growth based on the increasing needs of the population as it gets larger. These aren't hard and fast limits, as they were in *SimCity 2000*, but are essentially fluid changes in the needs of the city's population.

For instance, Residential demand may diminish if certain forms of recreation aren't available in your city. This occurs as your city's population grows and approaches the caps limit set by the simulation. Building a marina or a zoo can provide relief from that cap. In another example, a small Airport might serve the needs of a city of 50,000, but as the city approaches 1,000,000 Sims, the Airport will need to be expanded to meet caps on Commercial and Industrial demand—though Airports provide relief primarily for Commercial demand caps. Seaports provide some Commercial cap relief, but their benefit is mostly Industrial cap relief. You'll receive messages via news ticker and Petitioners to alert you to the problem.

If a city isn't desirable and demand is generally low, you must examine what is making the city less attractive. It might be excessive pollution or crime. Or, it might be that the taxes are too high, or the roads are too crowded. Sims are very demanding, and you'll have to be sure they have everything they need, or they'll tend to go elsewhere and your city will start to look like SimGhostTown. Improve the quality of life in your city, and the Sims will come.

Dealing with Pollution

Sometimes, especially in the early to mid-1900s, you end up with a lot of pollution. You must accept pollution as a fact of life in the early twentieth century, but that doesn't mean you can't minimize its effect on your city.

In the short term, there isn't much you can do to avoid pollution altogether. If you begin your city in the early 1900s, pollution is going to be a byproduct of industry, traffic, built-up zones, and specific buildings such as your power plant. However, pollution is generally a local effect, meaning you can minimize its effect on, say, Residential land values by keeping Residential zones away from big polluters like Industrial zones. So:

- Keep Residential and Commercial zones away from Industrial and other pollution sources. If possible, cluster all your polluting zones and buildings, including power plants and other major polluters, in their own areas of development as far as possible from your major centers of Commercial and Residential development.
- Build your most polluting buildings and zones near the edge of the map to cause some of the pollution to escape harmlessly away.
- Keep water pumps away from major sources of pollution to prevent polluting your water system and reducing the effect of your pumps.
- Use mass transit whenever possible to reduce car emissions.
- Some ordinances can help to reduce pollution in your city, though you must be careful with ordinances that restrict industry because you can legislate against polluting industries, but for a variety of factors (land values, the year) cleaner industries may not be able to develop. If you attempt to control pollution through ordinances, be watchful for industrial stagnation.

In the short run, these measures are the best you can do. In the long run, you can have a much more significant effect on pollution by achieving a switch from polluting industries to cleaner ones. To do so, you must increase the overall EQ of your workforce. You can also increase the LE of your city's Sims, though increasing EQ is more important. If you successfully bring overall EQ up in your city, cleaner industries will

287

begin to develop over time. By enacting ordinances that favor cleaner industries, you'll help to encourage that shift. As technology improves over the life of your city, cleaner options will present themselves until, by the early twenty-first century, your city should be essentially pollution free.

Reducing Traffic

It's amazing how that little one-horse town of yours can grow, but, then, if your city isn't growing, there might be something wrong. One of the side effects of growth is that the original infrastructure of your city isn't always up to the task of moving people around and supporting their needs. When you first build your city, you may have relied almost exclusively on roads, or maybe a combination of roads and rail. Soon, those roads become overcrowded. What can you do?

Create mass transit options: This is the most obvious solution to traffic problems. Build bus stops, rail stations, and subway systems. These solutions will alleviate a lot of your traffic problems quickly. But remember, your mass transit system will add a line item to your budget. Be sure to keep mass transit funded to avoid a strike. Pass the Subsidize Mass Transit Ordinance as soon as you can. It'll significantly increase use of mass transit and reduce road congestion.

Widen streets: Yes, you can do some urban renewal and turn those overcrowded roads into avenues to accommodate the increased traffic.

Build highways: For long-distance commutes or to connect far-flung areas of your city, build some superhighways. Your Sims will thank you.

Build alternate routes: When all else fails, give your Sims some alternative routes to get where they are going. If you've built your Industrial complex at the end of one narrow road, don't be surprised if the Sims experience gridlock on the way to and from work. Build an alternate route, and preferably some mass transit options, to relieve the pressure.

Increasing Land Values

Land value is the single most important factor that affects what gets built in your city. Developed land with higher value also provides more tax revenue, which in turn allows you to support a city of higher density. Determining land value is one of the most complex aspects of *SimCity*. There are many elements that go into land value calculations (see Chapter 6: Land Development and the RCI Model for more information). But there are some aspects of land value that are easy to understand. For instance:

- Land value tends to be higher on hills or land of higher-than-average elevation. This is true of all zone types.
- Land value also tends to be higher near water. Shoreline and beachfront property has extra value. Even water you plop on the map has a beneficial effect.
- Pollution reduces land value. Keep Residential and Commercial land away from heavy pollution. Land values will receive a bonus if their pollution levels are lower than average.
- Crime reduces land value. Be sure you have enough police coverage to keep crime to a minimum. Your land values will receive a bonus if they have lower-than-average crime.
- Your land can never reach high density development without water, so be sure all your land is receiving an adequate supply of water.
- Watch for NIMBY and YIMBY effects. Some buildings can increase land value—parks, fountains, schools, police stations, etc. Other buildings lower land value in the immediate vicinity—power plants, Water Pumps, strip malls, etc. Be aware, also, that some buildings have a NIMBY effect in addition to other negative effects. For instance, a power plant has a strong NIMBY effect in addition to the pollution it may or may not spew out.
- Land value tends to be higher near the "City Center." For a more thorough discussion of how the City Center is determined, see the chapter on "Land Development and the RCI Model."

To reach the highest land values possible:

- Try combining buildings with YIMBY effects (parks, marinas, reward buildings, etc.) with zones near water or hills.
- Create high-density development near the City Center, where land value is highest. As your city expands, the area of highest land value also grows, so you can have a thriving metropolis of skyscrapers clustered in its commercial center.
- Also, to minimize the effects of pollution, cluster your heavy polluting buildings and industry together at the edge of the map, away from your Residential and Commercial development.
- You may even want to ship out garbage and purchase power to further reduce the polluting effects of landfills, incinerators, and power plants.
- In the long run, work to increase your city's EQ so that more clean industry can develop, which will have an overall beneficial effect on land values.

Reducing Crime

Crime is the inevitable result of cramming more and more Sims into your city, but it's fairly easy to deal with. There are two basic ways to reduce crime:

- Build police stations and jails
- Enact ordinances

In the first place, the solution is obvious. Build enough police stations to cover your city with crime protection and enough jails to keep the perps off the streets. Remember, however, that each police station or jail will add to your monthly budget, so be ready to pay the additional cost of your Sims' safety.

Certain ordinances have the effect of reducing crime. The Junior Sports and Youth Curfew ordinances, for example, reduce crime and boost EQ. Kids get a positive outlet for youthful energy, with the additional benefit of keeping them off the streets and out of trouble after school. Another ordinance, Neighborhood Watch, affects only crime, but it's very effective, reducing crime throughout your city.

Still other ordinances can help reduce crime, although you might not have guessed they'd have that effect. For instance, the Conservation Corps' primary effect is for increasing clean industry demand and reducing pollution and garbage, but by keeping teenagers busy with positive activities and a sense of purpose, they also keep themselves "clean."

Obviously, the downside of all these ordinances is that they cost money. You have to ask yourself the question, "Can I afford them?"

If you're strapped for cash, by the way, and feel you can risk some additional crime, you could always turn your city into SimVegas by passing the Legalized Gambling Ordinance.

Reducing Fire Danger

Unless you turn Disasters off, your city will always face the danger of a devastating fire. The solution is simple: build Fire Departments. Also, be sure all your buildings and zones are receiving water, which reduces their flammability. If you provide adequate fire coverage (with the associated hit on your budget) and water to all your zones, your risk of fire should be substantially reduced, and fires that do break out will be quickly contained with minimal loss. Although it's of some benefit to place Fire Departments evenly throughout your city, your greatest benefit will come from dispatching fire crews to the scene of a fire. So the number of Fire Departments you have in your city is somewhat more important than their placement. The more fire crews you can dispatch to the scene of a fire, the more quickly it will be controlled. Of course, smaller fires will be taken care of quickly by local Fire Departments if the fire breaks out within the coverage area.

Dealing with Disasters

You have the option to turn Disasters off, which will make it easier to build a successful city. However, you can add challenge and a dimension of excitement to your city by leaving them on. If you turn Disasters off, you won't have to worry about fire, earthquakes, tornadoes, riots, or alien attacks—yes, you can get extraterrestrial visitations, and they aren't particularly friendly, though they will make decorative crop circles in the fields if you have farms.

Here are a few suggestions for handling disasters or for avoiding the worst effects:

- Build Fire Departments and be prepared to dispatch them to the scene of any fires that break out. You'll have one fire crew for each station you build, plus one extra bucket brigade. In case of fire, use them!
- Watch the news tickers for items about dogs or cats getting nervous and overeating, or low rumblings, which are forewarnings of an upcoming earthquake.
- Worried about earthquakes? Enact the Earthquake Resistance and Retrofitting Ordinance to reduce the amount of damage your city will incur.
- News ticker items about weird weather patterns may foreshadow a tornado.
- If you do see signs of an upcoming tornado, issue an early warning using the EWS (Early Warning System)—if you do, you'll be eligible for more Disaster Relief. To use the EWS, click on the Emergency button, then click on Warning Siren. Don't overuse it, though. If you sound a false alarm too often, your Sims will stop believing you and the EWS will be ineffective.
- If the aliens come, your best protection from serious damage to your city is to make sure you have one or more landmarks in your city. Aliens will always go after landmarks first. If there are no landmarks, the little buggers will cause mayhem on your most cherished (and expensive) structures like power plants, Airports, etc. And you were wondering what landmarks were good for besides eye candy?
- To avoid riots, keep crime levels low, unemployment low, and aura high.

Getting the Most from Your Water System

There are only a few simple rules to creating an effective water system:

- Place pumps near fresh water.
- Keep Water Pumps and Towers away from major pollution sources.
- Lay pipes throughout your city to create an even distribution of water.
- Be sure to have enough pumping sources to provide complete coverage so none of your city goes dry.

In addition, you can pass the Water Conservation Ordinance, but your Industrial sector won't be very pleased with it.

Increasing EQ

Your city will thrive if its population is well educated. To provide adequate education for your Sims, be sure you have enough schools and colleges to serve your population, placing new ones as your city grows. Also, place museums and libraries to keep your population at its peak mental efficiency. Finally, enact ordinances to further promote education:

- Pro Reading Campaign
- Junior Sports (also cuts crime)
- Youth Curfew (also cuts crime)

Remember, your city's overall EQ will ultimately determine the kind of industry that develops, in turn determining how great or not-so-great a place your city is to live.

Increasing LE

Your Sims will live longer if you provide adequate health care. Building hospitals will help, as will enacting certain ordinances such as:

- Free Clinics
- Community CPR Training
- Public Smoking Ban
- Crossing Guards (careful, also boosts traffic congestion)

However, one of the major causes of lower LE is pollution. So, in addition to the active steps you can take to provide the best health care your budget can afford, you should make all efforts to reduce pollution as well.

Making your Sims Happy—Increasing Aura

Sims like a nice, ordered city, with low crime, low pollution, plenty of water, great health care, thriving business, and lots of good recreation. In short, they want it all. So, you know what to do. Keep your city clean and productive, and provide rewards to your citizens in the form of various kinds of parks, zoos, ballparks, marinas, and other places that say, "This city isn't just efficient, it's fun, too!"

If you can do without Nuclear Power Plants and military base missile silos, the Nuclear Free Zone ordinance is another way to boost Aura.

If you do it all right, you'll avoid having eggs thrown at your statue and your SimCitizens will adore you.

Chapter 20
Summary of Tips

Throughout this book, we've made suggestions about how to get the most out of your city simulation experience. This chapter attempts to summarize the best tips, and introduces a few new ones as well.

- Build your polluting buildings and zones near the edge of the map to minimize the effects of pollution.
- Build in a corner to make it easy to connect with two neighbors as soon as possible.
- Make neighbor connections early to increase successful trips, to boost demand, and to allow Neighbor Deals to take place.
- Make intelligent Neighbor Deals. If you do it right, they can help you realize your city's goals.
- Keep Residential and Commercial away from Industrial to avoid the negative pollution and NIMBY effects that would drive down land values, and, ultimately, tax revenues.
- Use water and elevation to maximize land values. You get a substantial boost to base land value when you take advantage of proximity to water and building on higher-than-average land.
- Build bigger zones and use water, police, and parks to raise land values. Buildings will often be constructed even if part of the building is farther from transportation than the allowable distance. This way, you get more development with less transportation infrastructure. If buildings don't develop, put in water, parks, and police stations to bring up land value and reduce cumulative pollution effects.

- Start with low-density zones for the most part, and plan for future urban renewal. Zoning for higher densities early in the life of a city is a waste of Simoleons and will slow development.

- Use lower taxes to stimulate demand. Taxes are your friend, and tax revenues definitely grease the wheels of progress, but low taxes can bring up demand, which ultimately may result in even more revenue and growth.

- Turn off Disasters and you won't have to worry about fire or fire departments. Okay, it's sort of a dodge—a way to avoid your civic responsibility—but it sure makes the game easier to play.

- Hospitals really don't do much. As long as your Sims live long enough to be in the work force, they don't have to live to be 90. At least the hard-core players agree that you can pretty much dispense with hospitals.

- If you want to see the coolest buildings in the game, maximize your City Center effect and build a high-density Commercial zone there.

- Take Business Deals as long as you know how to combat their negative effects.

- Pass the Shuttle Ordinance and the Subsidize Mass Transit Ordinance as soon as possible. For the Shuttle Ordinance to take effect, you must place some sort of mass transit in your city.

- If you feel that your Sims aren't completing all their trips, try placing a very small area (maybe 2 × 2) of Industrial right next to or even inside a Residential zone.

- Be sure that your train stations can reach all three zones or some trips will fail.

- Remember that police stations, Fire Departments, hospitals, schools, colleges, libraries, and museums don't need power, water, or access to transportation.

- Remember that local pollution is cumulative. Try not to cluster a lot of polluting buildings and zones together. As we stated before (but it bears repeating), placing areas of no pollution, like parks or water tiles, can have a very beneficial effect on the local pollution average.

Appendix A
Tutorial for Acquiring, Retouching, and Implementing Height Maps for *SimCity 3000* Terrain Editing

For this task, you'll need the following applications:

- *Photoshop* or *Paintshop*
- *SimCity 3000*
- *WinZip*
- *DLGv32*, available via download from the U.S. Geological Survey (USGS) at no charge

Acquiring the Maps

1. First, do a worldwide web search for a DEM (Digital Elevation Model) of the area you want to work with. You might want to look for the information on the web site for the USGS (*http://edcwww.cr.usgs.gov/doc/edchome/ndcdb/ndcdb.html*)
The United States has been thoroughly mapped, so if you're looking for a U.S. city, you'll have no trouble finding geographical information. Unfortunately, this information isn't as easy to get for the rest of the world. Keep trying, though—you may get lucky.

2. Once you get to the USGS web site, look at the maps in the second category, which is 7.5-Minute Digital Elevation Model (DEM), SDTS format only.

3. Find the state, city, or area you want to download and click on it until you get the choice to download.

4. Download the file or files.

5. The next window should prompt you to save to disk. These files are compressed, so you'll need WinZip to decompress them.

6. When you finish downloading the file, double click on it and you'll see WinZip opening with a small window in front of it. Add the extension *.tar* at the end of the file in the line and click "OK."

7. Drag or extract the uncompressed file to your desktop.

8. Unzip each quadrangle into its own folder.

9. Open DLG and go to File/Open. Choose "*.catd" from the menu at the bottom, and open your document with this.

10. Once the document is open, go to "Open Control Center," then "Options." Select "Vertical Options," "Disable Lighting," and "Select Gradient Shader." Then go to "Shader Options," and set the "Gradient Shader" to high and low colors to black for low and white for high. Your map will be a gray-scale height map where white represents the highest elevation points and black represents sea level.

11. Make the entire landmass fit in the screen. Choose "Print Screen" and paste into your favorite paint or photo editing program.

Retouching

1. Open *Photoshop* or *Paintshop Pro*.

2. Paste the screen capture into the editor.

3. Go to "Image/Rotate Canvas/Arbitrary."

4. Type 45, and make sure the CCW or left is selected (this will rotate your picture to align the natural geographical north with the *SimCity* north).

5. Choose the rectangular selection tool from the tool menu.

6. Select a square around the area you want to use (make sure it's a square and not a rectangle) Each side of a large city terrain is about 10 miles long. Keep this in mind while selecting an area. DLG offers a measuring tool.

7. Use Ctrl C (Copy). Then Ctrl N (New). Click "OK," and then use Ctrl V (Paste). Close your big old document.

8. Set the image to a 256-shade gray scale image. Posterize the landform to make playable plateaus and terraces. Any color *over* 30 will be above water, all colors 30 and under are submerged. Use "Blur" to smooth out the terraces. Try not to have any pixels more than four shades off any adjoining pixels. Now tweak with the settings on the "Image/Adjust" menu. Try "Brightness/Contrast" and "Levels" until you get an image that doesn't contrast too much. Otherwise, you'll get very high mountains and low valleys when you apply it. Remember that white is very high and black is very low for altitude purposes, so you want a bitmap with lots of nice shades of gray that change gradually.

9. When you're done tweaking these settings, go to the "Layer/Flatten Image" menu option. This function will merge your top layer with the background.

10. Next, go to the "Image/Image Size" menu option. Uncheck the "Constraint Proportions" at the bottom of the window that pops up (this will allow you to change height and width).

11. Resize the image, type 257 (or 129), and make sure "pixels" is selected in the first and second lines of the window. The size of the BMP *always* has to be the grid size in *SimCity* plus one, so it's 256 + 1 or 128 + 1.

12. Click "OK."

13. Finally, go to the "Image/Mode" menu and choose "Indexed Color." Click "OK" in the next window.

14. Go to "File/Save As" and choose .bmp. Click "OK."

Implementing

1. Remember the name you gave your bitmap file. It's very important.
2. Open your game.
3. Choose "New Game" and the size of the map that matches your BMP size (either 256 × 256 or 128 × 128).
4. Open the cheat code window using the command [Ctrl] [Alt] [Shift] [C].
5. Type *Load Terrain c:\path\(exactname).bmp.* (Using the name of your document, including the *.bmp* extension).
6. Click "OK."

Appendix B
Cheat Codes

The programmers at Maxis have included hidden codes that will let you alter, ignore, and generally infringe upon the laws governing the *Sim City 3000* universe. Press Ctrl + ⇧Shift + Alt + C to bring up the cheat code window.

Feel free to search the Internet for even more cheats—but, as veterans of previous *Sim City* titles will tell you, there is a justice in this SimWorld. Crooked mayors of the past have laughed all the way to the bank only to witness, not long afterward, their city's destruction by giant lizards and flying saucers.

A Shady Relation Lends a Hand

For some under-the-table money, type "call cousin Vinnie." Then attend the "Local Fundraising Event" that now appears in the Meet window. The deal will net you 100,000 Simoleons in dirty money.

If you refuse to let Vinnie grease your palms with his filthy lucre, you will be rewarded for your scruples. You will receive a new code, "zyxwvu." The magic word will add a special castle to your Rewards list, a monument to your unshakeable principles.

Unearned Rewards

Type "I am weak," to build, zone, and landscape for free. Or, type "pay tribute to your king" to build all reward buildings.

Technology From the Future

"Garbage in, garbage out" makes all garbage buildings available, even if it's 1900. "Power to the masses" does the same for power structures, and "water in the desert" instantly lets you build every type of water building.

Modifying the Terrain

The cheat code "Salt on" lets you transform fresh water into salt; typing "salt off" does just the opposite.

"Load terrain" lets you load a grayscale image as terrain.

"Terrain one up" and "terrain one down" raises and lowers the entire landscape, although this may wipe out your city.

Secret Messages from the Programmers

Finally, typing each of the following codes causes a hidden message from the programmers to scroll across your news ticker.

* 1234
* advisor
* bat
* broccoli
* electronic arts
* erts
* hello
* help
* llama
* maxis
* mayor
* money
* moremoney
* sc3k
* scurk
* sim
* simcity
* ticker
* will wright

Index

groundwater. *See* water.

H

hardware, personal computer, 3

health. *See* LE (Life Expectancy).

Health, Education, and Aura (HEA) ordinances, 218, 222–223, 229–232

height maps, 297–300

high-density zoning, 42, 59–61

highways, 113, 114–115

hints, game, 29

Historic Preservation Zone, 27

historic/landmark buildings, 27, 29, 45, 73

home computers, 3

Homeless Shelters Ordinance, 226–227, 239

hospitals, 15, 190–193

housing, 10, 49

I

immigration, 180

implied transportation, 101–102. *See also* transportation.

importing/exporting garbage, 152–154, 156, 252–255, 261–264

incinerators, 150–152, 156

income, 210–213

Industrial Pollutant Impact Fee Ordinance, 226–227, 240

Industrial Waste Disposal Tax Ordinance, 156, 224–225, 234

Industrial zones. *See also* RCI.
  development of, 75–78
  effect of ordinances on, 78–79
  land value development thresholds, 70
  placement of, 38, 43
  supply and demand for, 10–11, 48
  transportation considerations, 71, 102

industry, clean *vs.* dirty, 15, 75, 77–70

intelligence. *See* EQ (Education Quotient).

interface, user, 25

Internet, 301

IQ. *See* EQ (Education Quotient).

J

jails, 14, 63, 178, 269, 271, 272

Job Fair ordinance, 79, 145, 226–227, 242

jobs, 10

Junior Sports Ordinance, 174, 189, 222–223, 229–230

L

land development
  coordination with game states, 23, 69
  RCI caps and, 57–58
  supply and demand, 48–51, 69
  taxation and, 53–57, 213
  zoning and, 51–53, 58–61

land value
  award building effects on, 276
  City Center Effect on, 66–68, 289
  development thresholds, 70
  formula for calculating, 68
  impact on tax revenues, 27, 55, 65, 68
  major factors affecting, 10–11, 62
  strategies for boosting, 65, 66, 289–290
  supply/demand and, 10–11
  terrain effects on, 36–37, 64–65
  water structures and, 127
  zone density and, 60

Landfill Gas Recovery Ordinance, 145, 224–225, 237–238

landfills, 59, 61, 149–150, 156

landmarks, 27, 29, 32, 45, 73

Lawn Chemical Ban Ordinance, 148, 224–225, 236

layers, 24, 280, 281
  Aura, 29
  Crime, 173, 174–175